BACKCOUNTRY
Fly Fishing
IN SALT WATER

BOOKS BY

CARL RICHARDS and DOUG SWISHER

► ◄

SELECTIVE TROUT

FLY FISHING STRATEGY

STONEFLIES (with Fred Arbona)

EMERGERS

BACKCOUNTRY FLY FISHING IN SALT WATER

BACKCOUNTRY
Fly Fishing
IN SALT WATER

*An Innovative
Guide to Some of
the Finest and Most
Interesting Fishing
in Salt Water*

• • •

DOUG SWISHER
and
CARL RICHARDS

Illustrated by Mike Gouse

LYONS & BURFORD, PUBLISHERS

Printed in the United States of America

Design by Howard P. Johnson
          Communigrafix, Inc.

10 9 8 7 6 5 4 3 2 1

Library of Congress Cataloging-in-Publication Data

Swisher, Doug.
    Backcountry fly fishing in salt water : an innovative guide to
some of the finest and most interesting fishing in salt water /
Doug Swisher and Carl Richards.
        p.   cm.
    Includes bibliographical references and index.
    ISBN 1-55821-328-7
    1. Saltwater fly fishing.   I. Richards, Carl, 1933–
II. Title.
SH456.2.S88   1994
799.1'6—dc20   94-45123
                                            CIP

Acknowledgments

A number of people helped us with this book and we would like to thank them for their efforts.

First of all, our thanks to Nick Lyons, our editor and publisher, who made the book possible; to Alecia Richards for editorial assistance and for putting up with frequent disappearances to the salt; to Robert Braendle, who did the color for the artificials and assisted us with collecting some of the prey; to George Germain for help with collecting specimens, keeping the boat running, and being a fishing friend; to Allen Fici, who helped us collect prey.

To Tim Fox and Jerry Klavins, besides being good friends, thanks for making it possible to fish the Golden Bonefish Lodge on Turneffe Reef and collect many creatures which have never been photographed. Thanks to Jim Bloom and Jim Ostead, who assisted us in collecting in the Bahamas. To Dr. David K. Camp, Dr. Richard Matheson, Mr. Peter Hood and Mr. David Pierce, of the Florida Marine Research Institute, who very graciously helped us with identifying prey species; to Bruce Willson and Larry Woods, who made both our boats possible.

To Sharon Chaffin and Don Phillips for their fly tying and photographic assistance.

And, a very special thanks to Bob Marvin for sharing with us his incredible knowledge of the salt.

BACKCOUNTRY
Fly Fishing
IN SALT WATER

Backcountry Fly Fishing—What It Is— Where To Find It— How To Find It

WHAT IT IS

Backcountry fly fishing, found mostly in salt water, is very exciting and can be described as shallow-water angling in an area bound on one side by an outside barrier island or islands, continuing back to the mainland and beyond. It can be enjoyed in uncrowded waters and is a good change of pace from crowded trout streams.

Backcountry includes coastal rivers, lakes, and canals when migrations of gamefish take them there. One location may have a long barrier island, a bay, and then the mainland. Another location may consist of many large and small outside islands between the barrier islands and the mainland.

Inshore and offshore saltwater fishing is practiced on the seaward side of barrier islands. Inshore (on or very close to the shoreline), and offshore (farther out than you can wade), cannot be completely separated from backcountry fishing because they blend into each other. Two very good examples of this

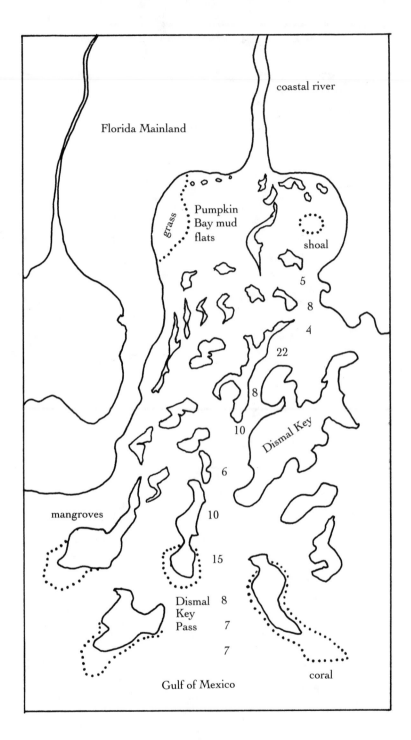

Example of many small barrier islands

blending are the snook and tarpon migrations offshore. During the spring, snook migrate from far inside the backcountry to the outside passes to spawn. They feed along the outside beaches when not spawning. Many times while migrating from the south, pods of giant tarpon will appear at dawn about a quarter-mile off the mouth of a coastal river or pass.

Backcountry destinations exist all over the world and it would take volumes to describe them all. We will list some of our favorite locations along with the primary targets you will find there and the best times to fish for them. Other species of gamefish are always present at these locations and these become targets of opportunity. Seasonally, secondary targets may become primary targets when large schools appear.

WHERE TO FIND IT

FLORIDA

Virtually the entire state of Florida has backcountry of one degree or another. By far the deepest (the distance from outside islands to the mainland) is the 10,000 Islands, which as a region probably has a lot more than 10,000 islands. Most of this area is a true wilderness. It stretches from Naples on the north to Florida Bay on the south and east. The primary targets are snook, tarpon, redfish, jack crevalle, and sea trout. The best fishing is from April to November, but all of the primary and many of the secondary targets can be caught all year. It would be impossible to name one pass or bay in these islands that does not hold gamefish, and the fly fishing is very good.

The Florida Keys stretch from Key Biscayne to Key West. Both the Atlantic and the Gulf side of the Keys are productive, but the Atlantic flats have more fish earlier in the spring. The primary targets are bonefish, permit, tarpon, and redfish. The bonefish in the Keys are very large, though wary, because the area is so heavily fished. The best times to fish are from April to June and from October to December. During very cool weather, barracuda will roam both backcountry and the outside flats and become a primary target.

The east coast of Florida, from Key West to the Georgia border and beyond, has backcountry, but it is not as deep and not as secluded. Snook, tarpon, redfish, and sea trout are the primary targets although snook are not found much beyond Cape Canaveral. June through October are the best months for fishing.

The Gulf side of Florida, north of Naples to the Florida panhandle, is loaded with clear, grassy flats, back bays, and passes where the primary targets are redfish, tarpon, and snook. Snook are not present north of Port Richey. Around the time of the first full moon in June, giant tarpon gather at the Boca Grande Pass west of Fort Myers to feed on the tons of bait swept out of Charlotte Harbor by the strong spring tides. The fish are so thick that they look like the bottom of the pass on a depth finder. The pass is 70 feet deep but many fish stray to the shallow waters where they can be hunted with a fly rod. The flats are very clear, so sight fishing for redfish occupies us most of the time in this area. But plenty of snook and sea trout are around, so you can take your pick. June through October are the best months for the primary targets.

Northwest Florida and the Florida panhandle also have some interesting backcountry. Many of the rivers feeding into the Gulf are spring-fed. This creates lush grass beds that attract spotted sea trout and redfish. Tarpon, along with sea trout and redfish, can be found in and around the passes during June, July, and August.

GULF COAST STATES

In addition to Florida, good saltwater angling is also found in Texas, Louisiana, Mississippi, and Alabama. Texas, because of its complete net ban, is especially good for redfish and sea trout. Port Mansfield, Texas, is a small isolated community north of Brownsville. It sits on the northern edge of the lower Laguna Madre. This is a vast shallow bay that is justifiably famous for its superb sight fishing for redfish and spotted sea trout. It has a firm grassy floor, so wading is the preferred means of stalking targets.

To the north lies the upper Laguna Madre, Redfish Bay, and the Aransas National Wildlife Refuge, all of which offer a variety of water, from open bays, closed bays, oyster reefs,

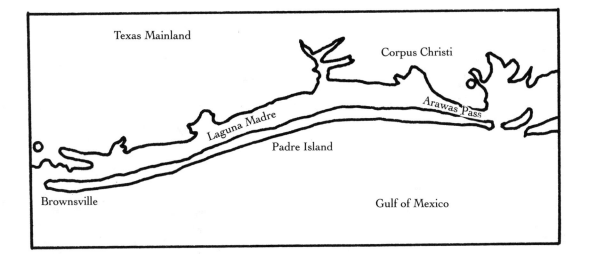

Texas Mainland

Corpus Christi

Laguna Madre

Arawas Pass

Padre Island

Brownsville

Gulf of Mexico

Example of a single-day barrier island

ponds, grass flats, and tidal creeks. The huge area from the lower Laguna Madre north to the Aransas National Wildlife Refuge has become a mecca for saltwater fly fishing—not only for redfish and sea trout, but black drum, jack crevalle, and flounder. The best times are June through September, though October can be very good as well.

Off the coasts of Mississippi, Alabama, and Louisiana, the islands and every major bay have good redfishing. Louisiana has a good fishery for giant tarpon, which show up in August and stay around until late September. Texas also offers some tarpon action from April through September, but it is mostly offshore.

ATLANTIC COAST STATES

The Atlantic Coast states all possess backcountry and close, inshore fly fishing. Bluefish and striped bass are the primary targets from Maine to Georgia in the summer. The New England coastline has thousands of small bays, tidal coves, and salt ponds where backcountry fly fishing is practiced. Long Island Sound, Cape Cod, and islands such as Martha's Vineyard all have great fishing in season. The primary targets are striped bass, bluefish, bonito, and false albacore. For stripers and blues, the best times are May and June, then September and October. July, August, and September are best for bonito and al-

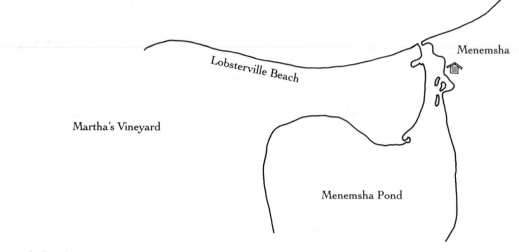

Lobsterville Beach

Menemsha

Menemsha Pond

Stripers on the beach

bies. These gamefish move north in springtime and south in the fall. The Georgia coast north to the Chesapeake Bay has some of the largest redfish on the planet. Late spring to fall is the best time to fish for them.

South Carolina possesses classic backcountry along most of its coast, and a relatively new fishery for this area is developing. The coast is a maze of coastal rivers and creeks with mud flats that are bordered by live oyster bars and grassy marshes. On the flooding tides, redfish move up onto the flooded marshes. Local anglers have recently learned to follow the reds with bonefish skiffs. Since commercial gill netting and trawling have been stopped, this state is, like Texas, a mecca for sight fishing to feeding redfish. The best times to fish the flats are fall and early winter when the fish school, but they can be caught all year.

MEXICO

Bonefish inhabit all of Mexico's eastern shoreline. The best angling, though, is located along the Yucatan Peninsula north of Cozumel to south of Belize. This area has an enormous amount of backcountry. Ascencion Bay alone may possibly possess more backcountry than the 10,000 Islands of Florida.

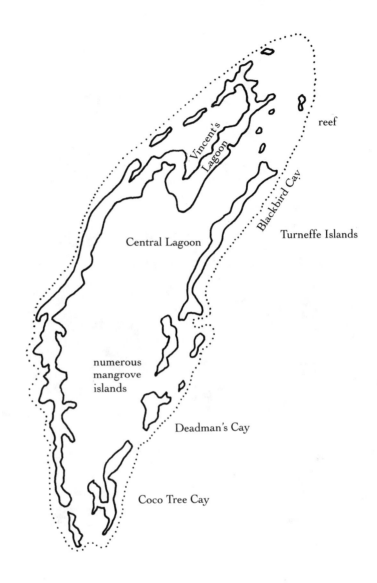

Vincent's Lagoon

reef

Blackbird Cay

Turneffe Islands

Central Lagoon

numerous
mangrove
islands

Deadman's Cay

Coco Tree Cay

Example of backcountry in Belize

Here the flats, unlike in the Bahamas, are mostly backcountry since they are behind the barrier islands. Bonefish are the primary target, but this area is probably your best chance for permit on a fly because permit are found on the deeper flats. Tarpon inhabit the outside beaches, the lagoons behind the barrier islands, and the mouths of the jungle rivers. Best times for fishing here are April through June and October through November.

Fabian, head guide of the Golden Bonefish Lodge in Belize, points to a school of bonefish coming up on to the shallows on the flooding tide for Sam Lacina.

THE BAHAMAS

The Bahamas are legendary for a plenitude of very large bonefish, plus good permit fishing and the occasional tarpon, shark, or barracuda. The bonefish on average are much larger than the Yucatan fish and are almost as plentiful. They are certainly far less "spooky" than the Florida fish. Seventy thousand square miles of almost deserted flats make this the world's largest and best location for bonefishing. The flats are mostly offshore, but many of the outer islands have true backcountry. The most notable are the Bights of Andros Island, where resident tarpon take flies well. Even the tiny Berry Islands have some backcountry, like the mangrove-lined Shark River of Great Harbour Cay. Here bonefish, along with permit, tarpon, shark, and barracuda, come in with the flooding tide. With the exception of bonefish, they can be caught all year. Bonefish can be caught all year depending on the weather, but the very best times are April through June and October through December.

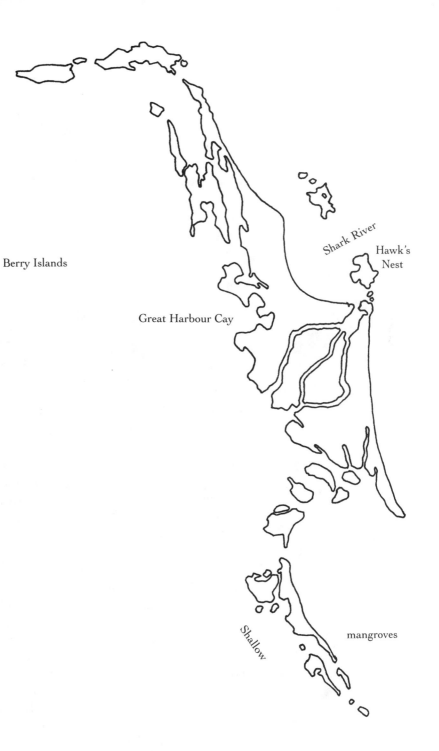

Berry Islands

Great Harbour Cay

Shark River

Hawk's Nest

Shallow

mangroves

Example of backcountry in the Bahamas

OTHER BACKCOUNTRY AREAS

A few of the more notable destinations for backcountry fly fishing are Christmas Island, with good fishing March through November; the Cayman Islands, with good fishing April through June and October through November; New Zealand, with good fishing February through April; Australia, with good fishing April through November; New Guinea, with good fishing April through November; East Africa and South Africa, with good fishing in January and February; Costa Rica, with good fishing January through June and September through October; Venezuela, with good fishing April through August and in November; and the British Virgin Islands, which have good fishing all year!

HOW TO FIND IT

Charts are vital in backcountry fishing, especially if you are out on your own. Most people will want to hire a guide for at least the first few times in a new area. This does become expensive, so much so that most people cannot afford to practice angling with a guide on a regular basis. In the spring of 1993, we fished the Berry Islands fully intending to use a guide—at least for a couple of days. The first morning of our trip, the "storm of the century" hit. The water became unfishable and it would have been a waste of money to have hired a guide. We had charts with us, so we rented a skiff and went exploring. By the time the conditions had improved we knew the water so well we didn't need a guide. By learning to read nautical charts, you can, on your own, find and fish backcountry anywhere, and do it with fewer dollars involved.

The first step is to go to a local marina and buy a large scale (1:40,000) nautical chart of the area you are interested in. By examining it, you will find areas of shallow water near shore on the barrier islands and inside the barrier islands. The depths are marked and the numbers will indicate low mean tide. If you locate on your chart some shallow flats with a deep hole nearby, you have probably found a hotspot. No charts are en-

Low incoming tide in Estero Bay with oyster bars exposed. This jack moved up on the bar and was feeding in six inches of water.

tirely accurate. There will be holes that are not marked on the chart, so you may need to do some exploring to find them. When you find an unmarked hole it usually will be a bonanza since few other anglers will know about it.

To thoroughly understand the charts you should have *U.S. Chart #1*, which is not a chart, but a book that explains the markings on charts. After studying the book and your chart you will understand where to go to find backcountry. The chart will also tell you where *not* to go. One example would be oyster bars. These are usually marked on charts and are good places to fish around but bad places to run your boat aground. You want to get to them, but you have to be careful when you get close. Another example would be if the chart says a bay is two feet deep—this means two feet deep at mean low tide. It may be dry at a spring low tide. Explore a new area at low tide. Go as slowly as possible and then you will know when and where you can run the boat at speed. An easy rule to follow when fishing backcountry is to not run your boat where you see birds walking!

After studying the chart and locating the backcountry, take the chart to a local fly shop, bait store, or a local fisherman. Ask them to mark good fishing places. Most people will be helpful. If you are fishing in southwest or southeast Florida, or the Florida Keys, you can buy eight different small-scale charts from *Florida Sportsman Magazine*. These charts have hot spots already marked. The smaller scale charts are not, however, very useful for navigation.

If you have a boat and you have studied your chart, you are ready to start exploring the backcountry. Anything from a one-man kick boat, a canoe, or a pram, up to a powerful bass boat, can be successfully fished. The shallower the draft of the boat the better because some of this fishing is in very "skinny" water. All boats are a compromise of one sort or another. Too shallow a draft and choppy seas will be impassable. If a hull was designed for very rough water, it will probably go aground in backcountry flats.

There are many places in the backcountry where a kick boat will be preferable to a bonefish skiff and becomes the practical choice. If you understand your chart and the tides, southwest Florida has many spots where you can launch a kick boat at a public landing and follow the incoming tide into the back bays, fishing as you go. When the tide turns, you simply fish with the flow of the ebbing tide back to your car. If you add a small electric motor or a tiny outboard to your kick boat, you will have much more range and versatility.

2

Tides

A complete understanding of tides is *the single most important factor* for consistent success when fishing for inshore gamefish. Weather and water temperature are important, but the tides determine the timing and intensity of feeding periods. Good tides create a banquet condition, much like a hatch on a trout stream initiates heavy feeding. When the water is moving well, it brings food to the waiting fish. The more powerful the current, the more baitfish, shrimp, crabs, and marine worms that are carried in the flow.

To be uniformly successful, the angler must understand what the stage of the tide will be when he plans a fishing trip, and he must be able to determine where the fish will be at that stage. After all, only three things can happen on a trip to the backcountry. One, you are where the fish are but they are not feeding. Two, fish are feeding but you are in the wrong spot. Three, fish are feeding and you are in the right spot. Knowledge of the tides will allow you to determine the time and location of number three.

Knowing where to fish and when to fish usually means great fishing. The "where to fish" part is not as difficult as you might imagine. In fact, it is somewhat obvious. At low tide, twenty-pound tarpon will not be roaming a flat in six inches of water. They will, obviously, be in deeper cuts and holes. When the tide turns and comes in, they will forage out of the deeper spots to feed on the myriad creatures that live in the shallow water.

The "when to fish" part of the equation requires the angler to completely understand tides and their causes. If you don't understand what the tide is doing and what it will do while you are fishing, you will never be able to plan *where* to fish.

Tides are the periodic rise and fall of the water level. They are caused by gravitational attraction of the moon and, to a smaller extent, the sun. The best tides occur on—and a few days on either side of—a full moon or a new moon. These are called spring tides. (This term has nothing to do with spring or fall seasons.) At these times, the sun and the moon work together to produce a greater swing between high and low tides. The greater the swing, the more powerful the current; the greater the current, the more food is swept in. The point between high and low tide when the current is strongest is called its *peak flow*. This is the moment when the most food is available.

On the first quarter and last quarter of the moon, the sun and the moon are at right angles to each other, so the gravitational forces are lessened; the tides are poorer, and are called neap tides. Lesser tides also have a peak flow period, but the flow is weaker and less food is available. If you are planning a trip to the backcountry, always try to hit the spring tides. You will almost always have much better fishing.

Wind can affect tides also. If the tide is coming in and the wind is pushing in the same direction, the tide will be higher than normal. If the wind is pushing in the opposite direction, the tide will be lower than normal. A very strong wind can actually kill a tide, or make it many feet higher than normal.

Barometric pressure can have an effect on tides, especially when the change is extreme. A high tide must rise against the weight of the air above it and a low tide is pushed down by that weight. When barometric pressure is high, high tides are not as high as predicted, and low tides are lower than predicted. When the barometric pressure is low, both the high and low tides are higher than predicted. In Florida, normal pressure changes will affect the predicted tides by about six inches, and

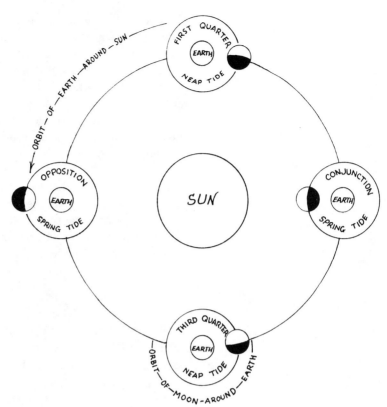

Drawing of the sun and moon illustrating how tides work, and spring and neap tides.

extreme conditions will affect them by about twelve inches. This can be of great significance if you are on a backcountry bay in ten inches at the predicted low tide. You could find your skiff aground if the wind or barometric pressure acts against you.

Different stages of the tides are as follows:

1. ***High*** The water is as deep as it is going to get and the current is slack.

2. ***Low*** The water is as low as it is going to get and the current is slack.

3. ***Outgoing*** High tide turns and the water is flowing out. This is also called falling or ebbing.

4. ***Incoming*** Low tide turns and the water is becoming higher. This is also called rising or flooding.

5. *Peak flow* The moment the current is at its swiftest. Peak flow (a very important term in backcountry fly fishing) occurs on both outgoing and incoming tides. The time interval between high and low tide is approximately six hours. Peak flow takes place at roughly halfway between high and low tides. Thus we have an outgoing peak flow and incoming peak flow. These are always best around the new moon and the full moon, and the weakest during quarter moons.

6. *Peak fishing flow* The period when the tide will be moving fast enough to produce excellent feeding. It is generally, but not always, the most productive time. It occurs approximately one and one-half hours on either side of peak flow and lasts about three hours. These three hours are going to be your most productive times on the water.

Tide tables are available at most marinas, tackle stores, and bait shops. They will list the time of high and low tides and usually how strong they will be. The tables are for a specific geographical area, usually the major pass in the region. For instance, if you pick up a tide table in Naples, Florida, the times listed will be for the mouth of Gordon Pass, the major pass in Naples. If you are fishing around Marco Island, fifteen miles south of Naples, you must subtract one hour from the tables to get the correct time for Big Marco Pass. The local sports shops will give you the corrections where you are fishing. You still must do some calculations for yourself, however. The times given on the tables are for the mouth of the pass, but the times will be later the farther inside the pass you go. For every mile you proceed inside the pass, the tides are twenty minutes later than the tables state. If you are five miles inside the pass, twenty minutes times five miles equals 100 minutes—a little less than two hours later than the tables.

Understanding this phenomenon can greatly extend your most productive fishing periods. Say you wish to sight-fish for reds from peak flow to low tide. You can begin fishing an outside bay just before peak flow and continue till dead-low. You would then quickly run (a good reason for a fast boat) to an inside bay three to six miles into the backcountry and extend your fishing time one or two hours.

A mangrove bay at low tide with oyster shells exposed. On the flooding tide, redfish will move in and feed on the porcelain and mud crabs that live under the shells.

There are exceptions to everything and here is one: In the Gulf of Mexico, from Florida around to Texas, the tides have a three-foot fluctuation, so we fish with the spring tides. In Georgia and the Carolinas, the tides have a nine-foot fluctuation. The backcountry mud flats there have no grass, but are very fertile, and spotted sea trout grow to extraordinary size. During spring tides, the estuaries become extremely muddy, so here we fish the neap tides with their lesser flows and clear water. Local knowledge is always necessary.

The "where to fish" part of the equation is mostly common sense if you keep these four simple factors in mind:

1. Strong outgoing tides sweep baitfish and crustaceans out of shallow bays, flats, creek mouths, and coastal rivers into the holes, cuts, and passes.
2. Strong incoming tides bring food from the open gulf or ocean into the passes and ultimately to the inside bays.

3 Gamefish will work up shallow bays and flats as the tide rises to feed on the creatures that live there. They will also move into the mangrove roots to feed on crabs, shrimp, and baitfish that hide around the oyster clumps at the bases of these roots.

4 Gamefish will move off the shallow areas to deeper cuts, points and creek mouths as the tide falls, where they waylay the forage swept out of the shoal zones.

Here are some examples of applying fishing tactics to tidal movements:

Small (ten- to fifty-pound) tarpon and other gamefish live around the inside bays all year in many areas, from Florida to South America and east to the Bahamas. These fish are non-migratory at this stage in their life cycle. At low tide they will congregate in the deeper cuts and holes. When the tide comes in, they will slowly move out towards the center of the shallow bays and flats to feed. Usually the deeper water will be at the mouth of the cuts or creek channels and the shallow zone will be in the center of the bay. Your tactic should be to arrive shortly after dead-low tide and position your boat between the deep cut and the shallow zone. As the water level rises, tarpon will work their way up towards the crest of the bar, usually showing themselves as they travel. You can position your boat into casting position with a quiet electric motor. When in place, cast three or four feet in front of the cruising fish. As the water level rises, the fish will move farther and farther out on the shallow bay. This fishing usually lasts for one and a half to two hours, until finally the water level rises so high that the fish are spread out all over the bay. If it's a small bay, you may still fish them successfully, but if it's a large bay they will be so dispersed that it would be luck if you got close to them. Later, after high tide, as the water begins to flow out, the tarpon will funnel back to the resting area. They can again be intercepted as they retreat to the deep hole at the cut. It must be noted that fish are much more inclined to strike when they are moving on the flat or bar, but when moving off, they can be in a great hurry. These are exactly the same tactics you would use for bonefish or permit on a flat, and snook and spotted sea trout have similar feeding habits on shallow, grassy areas and outside beaches.

Giant snook spawn in the outside passes in the summer, usually at night under a full moon. They feed, however, on the

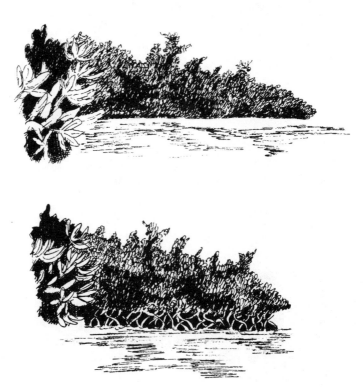

High and low tide on the same mangrove shoreline.

outside beaches in the surf near the mouths of the passes. As the incoming tide raises the water level up the intertidal zone (the zone between high and low tides) where many food forms live, snook feed higher on the beach. On the strong outgoing tide, snook will retreat to the nearby passes, cuts, and points because food is washed out from the shallow inside bays to the pass on the outside. Snook and other gamefish will lie there in wait.

At high tide around mangrove islands, many fish are far back in the roots and impossible to reach. Sometimes "popping the groves" will entice them out for a look-see. Later, at some point as the tide begins to fall, they must leave the mangrove roots and return to open water. These falling, but moving, tides are the time to sight-fish for reds and snook in the inside bays. Fish are coming off the shallow middle zone and out of the mangrove roots. The place to look for them is the deeper channels next to the bank.

Fishing periods of peak flow is especially productive around any type of structure. A point will serve as an ambush spot. Bridge abutments, rock jetties, and dock pilings are all good. Fish hang around these shelters, lying in wait for the cornucopia of food that strong tidal flows bring. Fishing lighted docks, bridges, and jetties can be particularly productive at night during peak flow periods, notably during spring tides when jack crevalle, snook, tarpon, and large ladyfish often engage in feeding frenzies.

Although incoming and outgoing peak flows produce outstanding feedings, choose outgoing tides if you can. There are local and seasonal exceptions, so be sure to get advice at local tackle shops. Another good source for information on local conditions will be baitfishermen. They know what's going on, are friendly, and will usually tell you everything you need to know.

In most all cases, feeding and movement of fish are determined by tidal stages and strength. Fish choose areas where tides will help them get as much food as possible. The fanciest flies and the most expensive tackle will not enable you to hook these fish if you do not understand what the tide is doing and how gamefish react to it. You will be infinitely more successful if you have a clear and deep knowledge of tidal movements.

An angler fishing a lighted dock at night.

Habits of Backcountry Gamefish

I n this chapter we will discuss some of the habits of backcountry gamefish as they relate to finding and hooking them. The primary species in the waters we fish are snook, tarpon and baby tarpon, redfish, sea trout, jack crevalle and pompano, bonefish, and permit. The secondary targets are snapper, barracuda, sheepshead, ladyfish, mackerel, bluefish, and sharks. Secondary targets can become primary targets seasonally and many of them are good fighters. Species like barracuda are around all year and can be specifically targeted. Tripletail are available but are not abundant. On the middle and north Atlantic coasts, striped bass are the primary target.

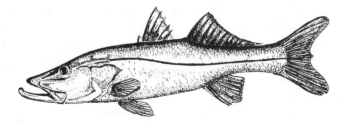

Snook

PRIMARY
TARGETS

Tropical and Subtropical
Fisheries

SNOOK

The best snook fishing is found in Florida south of Tarpon Springs on the west coast, and south of Cape Canaveral on the east coast. The average size is about five pounds, but thirty pounders are not uncommon and forty-pounders-plus are available. Snook rank with bonefish and tarpon as a gamefish, and the locals of southwest Florida rank them number one. Some very fine snook fishing can also be found on the eastern Mexican coast south to the Yucatan and along the Costa Rican beaches.

The important habits of snook for the backcountry angler to understand are the spring spawning migration and their intolerance of cold water. During the summer months they will spawn at night in the passes under a new or full moon. When not spawning, they feed along the beaches and bays near the passes. They are structure-oriented, so you will find them around bridges, pilings, docks, etc. Snook prefer 75° to 87° water. They will rarely feed if the water temperature drops below 70° and will die in temperatures below 60°. These simple facts are very important for us to keep in mind because in winter the water often drops below 70° in south Florida and snook move to find warmer water.

It is now thought that some very large snook move offshore around wrecks and artificial reefs when cold weather arrives. They usually move up coastal rivers and canals, sometimes very far up. They have been taken on the Caloosahatchee River as far up as Lake Okeechobee. Snook like brackish water, but even fresh water will not stop their fall migration. Some of the best places to find them in winter are in the far backcountry of the Florida Everglades.

In the spring as the water warms, the fish will gradually move out of the backcountry and offshore reefs to the passes. Here the tidal currents will bring tremendous amounts of food

A nice snook caught by
Dave Ferrie

to them. The same tides support the eggs that the snook have
laid, and carry the fry into the back bays where they mature in
relative safety. This spring migration usually begins in April. In
the fall after the spawn and with cooling waters, they gradually
move back inside and perhaps offshore. This movement begins
in late November or early December, and by late December
they can be far up into the coastal rivers. When the mature
snook are moving toward the passes, they can be found anywhere from the mouths of coastal rivers all through the mangrove bays to the outside beaches.

TARPON & BABY TARPON

One of the most spectacular gamefish of the backcountry is the baby tarpon. These juveniles range from five to fifty pounds and are always available except during winter. It is vital to understand their habits because they will be found in places you would think impossible. If we do not understand how they get there, we can't find them.

Tarpon spawn offshore, possibly miles off in the open Gulf. The juveniles are somehow carried to inshore waters where they then move to the far backcountry—up rivers, creeks, and freshwater canals. On the highest spring tides of the year, which will flood areas normally dry, they move even farther back. In these protected areas they are safe from most predators as they slowly mature. Since tarpon can breathe air, they are not bothered by oxygen-poor water. They can be found flourishing in stagnant roadside canals like those bordering the Tamiami Trail. At some point when they become large enough, they take the flooding tides back out to the open salt.

After mature fish reach the open Gulf, exactly where they go on their migration routes is somewhat of a mystery. If, for instance, giant tarpon are in Central America in the winter, they may head directly across the Gulf to the Keys, then up the east and west coasts of Florida in the spring. We know that some do travel in this manner but some may also follow the Mexican coast around to Texas and Louisiana. Tarpon that appear in Central America could possibly have been hatched in Africa, and Florida's tarpon may have been hatched in Central America. We look for five- to fifty-pound fish everywhere all year and explore coastal rivers all the way to the outside passes and lagoons. Some large (fifty-pounds-plus) tarpon appear to be nonmigratory, but for the most part schools of giant tarpon (over 100 pounds) first appear in the southern Florida Keys in late February.

The water temperature they prefer is 75° to 85°, but their tolerance is 64° to 104°. As winter water warms in the spring, we look for the first schools on the flats at 70°. As the water becomes warmer, the tarpon schools move up the Gulf coast past the 10,000 Islands to Boca Grande Pass and the Homosassa area. Here they feed heavily at the mouths of the passes on forage swept out of the bays by powerful spring tides. It is thought

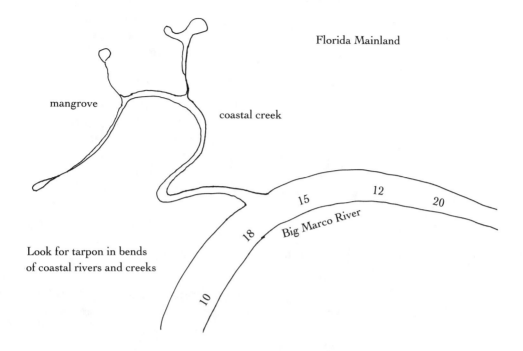

Florida Mainland

mangrove

coastal creek

15   12

18   Big Marco River   20

Look for tarpon in bends
of coastal rivers and creeks

10

Examples of Where to Find
Tarpon in Backcountry

that tarpon then proceed to the open Gulf to spawn. As fall approaches, they retrace their spring migration back to the 10,000 Islands, the Keys, and Central America.

REDFISH

The best angling for redfish occurs from Chesapeake Bay to the Carolinas and on south to Florida Bay, then up the Gulf from southwestern Florida to Texas. They are a superb gamefish whose habits lend themselves to sight-fishing in very shallow water. Redfish can tolerate colder water than snook or tarpon can. Some remain in the backcountry all year, but many will move offshore or up coastal rivers in the winter. The best fly fishing for redfish in Florida is from August through November when they school in shallow bays and flats. Spring fishing from March through June can be very good also. The lower St. Johns River fishes well in the winter. The summer rains bring fresh water to the backcountry of the 10,000 Islands, so many reds migrate to the outside islands and passes. The Indian River Lagoon on the east coast offers good fishing all summer. In the winter, if the water drops below 60°, feeding drops off dramatically.

Redfish do not travel far from their home waters. They spawn in water warmer than 72° from August through November, with November being the peak time. Spawning takes place in the open Gulf or in the Atlantic near shore and in passes and bay mouths. In large bays they often spawn in the bay itself. Like snook, reds spawn most heavily around the new and full moons.

SPOTTED SEA TROUT

These fish are very temperature-sensitive, preferring waters between 65° and 76°. This makes them a much better winter fish than snook and tarpon. Extremes above or below this range will drive them off the shallow grassy flats they prefer toward deeper water.

The sea trout's range is from Chesapeake Bay south and around the Florida Keys to the Yucatan. In Florida, spawning takes place from April through September when the water temperature reaches 75°. Spawning stops if the temperature exceeds 86°. It takes place mostly at night in channels and potholes in the flats adjacent to their grassy feeding areas. The big spawners can be taken on just about any type of fly from surface poppers to bottom-bouncing patterns.

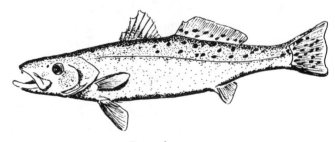

Spotted sea trout

JACK CREVALLE AND POMPANO

Florida pompano

These fish are very common in the backcountry and luckily are much less temperature-sensitive than snook and tarpon. In the winter during a cold snap, they can and often do save the day. The Florida pompano are abundant around inlets and sandy beaches. The jacks are found in mangrove bays as well as around artificial reefs. The only habit we need to be concerned with in angling for these fish is their gluttony. You name it, they eat it. Popping bugs with a dropper tied on may be the most deadly setup for them. Very small fish (two to three pounds) often astonish anglers who have never hooked one with their strong fighting qualities.

A very large jack crevalle taken in February five miles inside the outer pass in Estero Bay

BONEFISH

Bonefish live in all tropical seas. They will appear on the flats in the greatest numbers when the water temperature reaches 72° to 85°, although the larger ones will feed in cooler water. They are bottom feeders with the ability to crush clam shells, one of their favorite foods. They will consume most all marine invertebrates and the larger fish will take some baitfish.

Although some researchers believe bonefish spawn offshore in deep water, the latest thinking is that spawning takes place in inshore lagoons during high tide. It was reported that spawning bonefish found in lagoons were difficult to spook and very easy to hook.

PERMIT

The best fishing for the finicky permit is in Florida, the Bahamas, and eastern Mexico. They are found generally where bonefish are found, but usually in deeper water. These bottom feeders seem to prefer crabs, but it is thought they consume a considerable amount of snapping shrimp and mantis shrimp.

Permit spawn offshore in deeper water in the late spring and can tolerate warmer water than bonefish can. Very little is known about their travels, but schools of very large (forty-pound) fish show up over wrecks and artificial reefs off the southwest Florida coast in the summer. There is normally a big run of small (two-pound) permit into Sarasota Bay in the summer also. Nobody seems to know why either phenomenon occurs.

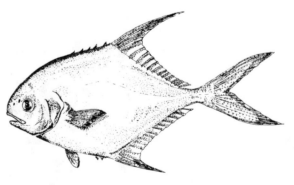

Permit

SECONDARY TARGETS

Tropical and Subtropical Fisheries

SNAPPER

There are 180 species of this family and most live in shallow water. The most popular snapper for fly fishing in Florida is the gray or mangrove snapper, but they are a very wary fish. They are usually caught around mangrove bays when one is fishing for snook and redfish, and will put up a good scrap. Mutton snapper are also found in the shallow-water flats of Florida and the Bahamas, and take a fly well.

A mangrove snapper

BARRACUDA

During the winter months, barracuda cruise the flats of the Florida Keys and the Bahamas. They are especially prevalent in the winter when other targets are scarce. Shrimp are not a very effective bait, but small silvery streamers are. Barracuda are superb leaping fighters, so a lot of anglers make them their primary target. Large barracuda migrate north in summer following the warmer 74° water and return south in the fall. They stay around all winter and they provide a fine sight-fishery.

Barracuda

SHEEPSHEAD

Another good winter fish, present in the backcountry when other species are not, are sheepshead. They like structure such as rocky bottoms, close-in reefs, wharves, and breakwaters. During their spring spawning season they move into shallow backcountry bays where they can be found tailing like bonefish. Sheepshead are bottom feeders and prefer small crabs and other shellfish. Small mud-crab imitations simulate their natural food.

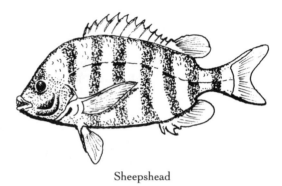

Sheepshead

LADYFISH

These fish are closely related to tarpon, and size for size probably outfight them. Ladyfish are abundant in south Florida and the Caribbean and inhabit shallow inshore waters, traveling in large schools. They feed heavily on sardines and shrimp, but seldom reach five pounds.

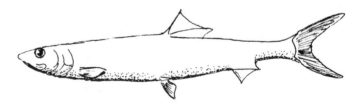

Ladyfish

MACKEREL

King mackerel are occasionally near the beaches in south-western Florida. Spanish mackerel are more numerous in the backcountry, where they often enter bays and passes. Both migrate north in the summer and south in the winter. They strike baitfish imitations well, but can be selective feeders on occasion. Mackerel will take baits from top to bottom, so it is best to fish all levels when you find a school.

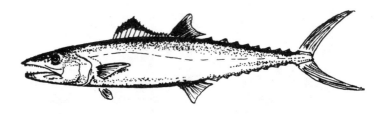

Spanish mackerel

BLUEFISH

The bluefish is another species that migrates north in summer and south in winter. They, along with striped bass, are the primary targets of the anglers of our northern Atlantic coast. Blues are not usually considered backcountry fish, but they often feed in water less than three feet deep. Small baitfish are their primary diet. In clear water they can provide good sight-fishing.

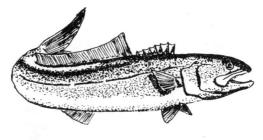

Bluefish

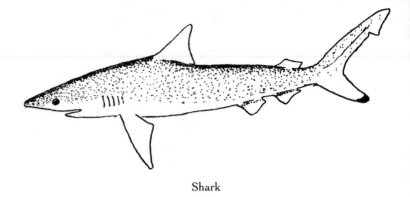

Shark

SHARKS

Because they take flies with some consistency, sharks can be an exciting target of opportunity in backcountry and flats angling. Like barracuda, you must target them specifically—both species have teeth and wire leaders are necessary. The black-tip shark is common in the Gulf and in the Caribbean. They roam inshore and like to eat scaled sardines. Lemon sharks also live inshore, mostly on bonefish flats, and take flies well. The best fishing for most species is during warmer weather, although they can be caught in winter. Sharks on bonefish flats like small bonefish, and good imitations are effective.

PRIMARY TARGETS

Temperate and Cold-water Fisheries

The primary targets of the cold-water Atlantic seacoast from Maine south to Chesapeake Bay are striped bass, bluefish, bonito, and false albacore (little tunny). This is a spring, summer, and fall fishery, and timing is important to intercept the northward spring movement and southward fall migration.

STRIPED BASS

The premier gamefish species of the northern Atlantic coast is striped bass. They winter in sanctuaries such as Chesapeake Bay and the Hudson River. When the water temperature climbs to 48°, they begin feeding and moving north along the New England coast. Their preferred temperatures are 55° to 64°. As they move north, they feed heavily on Atlantic herring, menhaden, Atlantic silversides, white mullet, and sand eels (American sand lance). They are best fished at night in the summer, but daytime fishing is good in spring and fall. They are a very strong fish and will feed close to shore in very heavy surf. Striped bass arrive in good numbers during May in Long Island Sound and during the month of June at Cape Cod and Martha's Vineyard. The southward migration begins in September for the Cape and Vineyard, and in October for Long Island Sound. By late November, the stripers will be back in the Hudson River and other like areas.

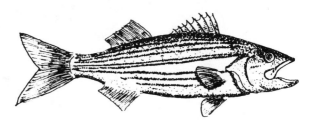

Striped bass

BLUEFISH

These fish range from Maine to Florida, migrating north in spring and south in winter. They prefer water temperatures from 61° to 68° and feed on the same baitfish as striped bass do. They start moving north in early March, arriving in Long Island Sound in mid-May, at Cape Cod and Martha's Vineyard in June, and a little later in Maine. By mid-November, most blues will be south of Long Island Sound.

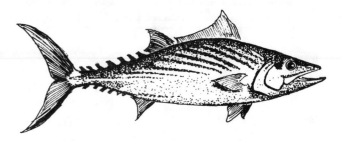

Bonito

BONITO AND FALSE ALBACORE (LITTLE TUNNY)

These fish, members of the mackerel family, move inshore in the summer and early fall when they feed on schooling baitfish such as sand eels and Atlantic silversides. They prefer moving water, so the mouths of bays and harbor openings (when tidal rip is at peak flow) are the areas to fish. Both fish are favorite northern targets since they are strong and incredibly fast. They seem to prefer warmer waters, as they do not appear until late summer and early fall.

Little tunny

Preferred Forage of
Backcountry Gamefish

Each species of gamefish seems to have decided food preferences. Often they will take what is available in the greatest numbers—but not always. They may just like the taste of certain fish or invertebrates, but it is pretty much taken for granted by locals that they prefer one type of food over others if given a choice. Permit seem to be the most specific when feeding. While other gamefish may have two, three, or more favored prey, permit relish crabs. It doesn't seem to matter if it's a blue, green, reef, or mud crab (whatever is locally abundant); put one in front of a permit and it's likely he will eat it. They will take shrimp on occasion, but all the really good bait-fishermen use crabs for permit if they can get them.

All gamefish eat the most nutritious prey for the least expenditure of energy. They zero in especially on whichever food source has the richest concentration of calories for the size of the fish or invertebrate. Bonefish like shrimp of various species. Permit prefer blue crab; snook love scaled sardines. All three of these forage species are very rich food sources. It may be that, over time, the gamesters developed a liking for prey that nourished them the most, and was available in their range, but for whatever reason, fish seem to have favorites.

Prey availability varies in both numbers and variety according to different substrates such as oyster beds, grass flats, silt bays, sand, and so forth. Mud crabs and small needlefish are numerous around many of the mangrove islands, while blue crabs swarm around river and creek mouths and grassy flats. Sardine species in the 10,000 Islands appear in huge schools around the outside passes, and along the bays bordering the passes. Gamefish feed accordingly. Changing seasons also play an important role in prey availability. The scaled sardines appear in the spring and swarm in the backcountry all summer only to disappear in the fall. Snook love them, but during cold weather you should be using a different imitation. Since the sardines are absent, they can't be fed upon!

Certain prey, such as shrimp and crabs, migrate from the outside depths to the shallows inside nursery bays. When mature, they migrate back again. These movements greatly affect food availability. When these migrations take place, huge numbers of very nourishing prey are passing by gamefish. As you would imagine, the gamefish feed heavily and selectively at such times.

In Florida's 10,000 Islands and the Florida bays backcountry, snook, small tarpon (twenty to sixty pounds), and redfish are considered the premier gamefish. We needed a good selection of effective fly patterns for these fish when we began fishing this area. The sheer numbers of saltwater flies recommended in literature and sold in shops were overwhelming, especially when we noticed the prices. The cost of one saltwater fly can vary from as little as four dollars to as much as fourteen dollars. These prices were staggering to someone used to trout patterns. Many saltwater streamers have the shape of a needlefish or halfbeak. They incorporate vivid colors of every conceivable hue, but most bear very little relationship to any needlefish in nature. Some patterns resemble shrimp, but the most realistic ties are coated with epoxy cement and are as hard as a rock, a characteristic we consider unacceptable.

A few patterns are tied to imitate crabs—presumably blue crabs, since they are a big favorite of permit—but when compared to immature natural blue crabs they are the wrong shape and color. Surprisingly, all these flies did catch fish, but often they were refused by actively feeding fish, even during feeding frenzies. Lefty's Deceiver is one of the glaring exceptions. This pattern, designed by Lefty Kreh, has an excellent baitfish shape and is easy to cast. It is probably the most-used saltwater fly in North America, and when dressed in realistic baitfish colors is deadly on most gamefish.

Other than the Deceiver and a few others, there is a bewildering variety of shapes, sizes, and colors to choose from and precious little reason to pick one pattern over the other. More than in self-defense than anything else, we decided we would learn the favorite foods of each species of gamefish and then try to tie realistic patterns to imitate them. This would greatly reduce the number of patterns and give us a logical starting point when choosing an imitation to tie on the end of the leader.

We learned that each type of fish does indeed have a decided preference in foods. Most of our literature states saltwater fish are opportunistic in their feeding habits, so exact imitations are not necessary. A few writers add, almost as an afterthought, that it is not a bad idea to carry a few flies which closely resemble the forage fish, as occasionally a correct imitation is critical. It made more sense to us to *start* with a realistic pattern. If they are feeding opportunistically, they should hit a close imitation, and if they are feeding selectively, they would certainly take the natural-appearing fly over the unnatural.

The late A. J. McClane reported he once found a single bonefish to contain forty snapping shrimp of a specific species. He said that looked suspiciously like selective feeding to him. We once came upon a school of tarpon just inside Big Marco Pass that appeared to be gorging themselves on threadfins. We had no pattern that resembled these baitfish, and our standard tarpon patterns were refused. After a few similar experiences we came to believe realistic patterns couldn't hurt, and definitely have the potential to greatly increase success.

We prepared a list of every important gamefish in the area with their four or five top food preferences. Tarpon under eighty pounds, for instance, love select white shrimp but also will not turn down a plump finger mullet, a blue crab, or a nice pinfish. Usually more than one favorite food was necessary for each gamefish. Once we had the finished list, we attempted to develop truly realistic patterns, as close to exact imitations as possible. The main objective was to create flies which were superrealistic but did not use rigid materials such as epoxy or hot glue to achieve the correct shape. Such construction simplifies tying, but results in a fly that feels like granite and casts like lead. Most anglers agree such patterns do not fish in a lifelike manner, and are rejected much more rapidly than resilient ties.

FAVORITE FORAGE OF SNOOK

Since snook are usually the preferred target of anglers in the backcountry of the 10,000 Islands, we began our research with them. One of the very best methods of discovering favored baits is to observe and question local baitfishermen. Some of these guys are really shrewd and they know what works. We asked them, and the snook specialists almost invariably answered whiting (white bait or shiners, or bull shiners, or crickets). This got a little confusing, but it boiled down to the fact that these names are all local terms for the same forage fish, the scaled sardine (*Haregula jaguana*). These are small, elegant, silvery fish with a darker dorsal. They are very delicate, flat-sided, and shadlike, with a deep belly and a flatter dorsal. They range in size from one-and-a-half to four inches, but one and-a-half to three inches are the best sizes for imitation in the backcountry. They are a member of the herring family, as are Spanish sardines and threadfin herring, all of which are relished. All possess similar shapes and coloration. These calorie-rich fish, if not always first, are very high on the preferred list for most inshore gamefish, with the exception of the bottom feeders.

The following is a list with descriptions of backcountry gamefish preferences. This list is somewhat subjective, as very little scientific work has been done on this subject except for bonefish.

1. **Scaled sardines** *(Haregula jaguana)* to five inches.
   RANGE: from Florida, the Gulf of Mexico, Bahamas, to Brazil, the same approximate range as snook. They appear in the spring in huge schools, and

stay around all summer, only to disappear in late fall. When they run in springtime, snook and other gamefish will engage in feeding frenzies, becoming extremely selective to exact size and shape. If gamefish are feeding on a school of one-and-a-half inch sardines, a two-inch artificial will be refused.

COLOR: green back with silvery sides and white belly.

2. **Bay anchovy** *(Anchoa mitchilli)*
Quite often during the warm months a smaller baitfish, the bay anchovy will swarm with the scaled sardines, especially at night under lights. Most individuals are three quarters of an inch long. Large snook and tarpon to forty pounds and other gamefish will feed on this tiny prey instead of sardines. Various small, close imitations are also needed. Over 150 species of anchovies are known. They are all so similar that they are difficult to distinguish. They are very abundant in tropical, subtropical, and temperate coastal waters. Most species prefer shallow backcountry bays, exactly where we prefer to fish.

COLOR: dusty gold back, silvery sides, with a white belly.

3. **Shrimp** Snook love southern commercial swimming shrimp *(Penaes* species). Three species: a) Pink *P. ∂nuranum)* b) Brown *(P. aztecus)* c) White *(P. setiferus)*.

SIZE: to six inches.

RANGE: Virginia to South America and Caribbean. The colors implied by the names are not reliable. Young specimens are translucent gray with delicate brown or dark gray markings called chromatophores. The eggs are laid offshore, and the young drift inshore with the incoming tide to mature in inside grassy bays and sounds. Mature shrimp return to the sea with strong outgoing tides. The largest migrations in Florida occur in summer and fall but some drift through the passes all year. Snook and other gamefish feed heavily and selectively on the migrations.

4. **Crabs**
   (a) **Common blue crab** *(Callinectes sapidus)* is the most abundant species.

   SIZE: to three-and-a-half inches long and twice as wide. The best sizes for fishing are smaller; #8, #6, #4, #2 for imitations.

   RANGE: Eastern Seaboard, Gulf of Mexico to West Indies. This is a swimming crab (family *Portunedae*). The hind legs of this family have evolved into swimming paddles and

Anatomy of a crab

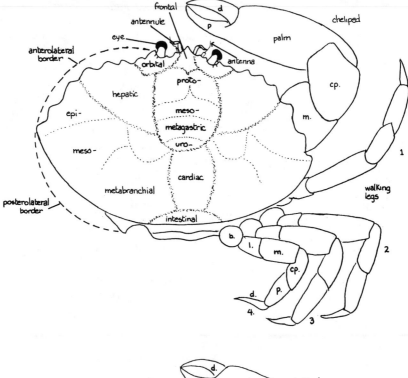

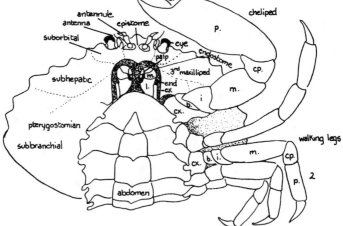

they are capable of very rapid movement. There are a number of similar species—they deposit their eggs in deeper salt water—but young crabs migrate to inside bays and river mouths to mature, and gamefish feed on them there. On outgoing spring tides, especially in May and June, these crabs often drift from the inside bays through passes, where large snook and tarpon lie in wait.

COLOR: (immatures) top is fawn to tan to brown to grayish blue-green with a white underside.

(b) Mud and Stone Crabs (family *Xanthida*)

SIZES: to three and-a-half inches for many species, including Black-and-White Fingered Crabs, and Stone Crabs.

RANGE: this family is common and widespread, ranging from Massachusetts to South America, the Gulf of Mexico and the Bahamas.

HABITAT: backcountry areas around mangrove roots and oyster bars.

COLOR: top, dirty tannish brown; underside, dirty cream.

(c) Fiddler Crabs (Genus *Vea*), many species

SIZES: two-fifths-inch to three-quarter-inch long.

RANGE: southern U.S., Gulf of Mexico, Bahamas, to South America.

HABITAT: mangrove islands, backcountry beaches, river mouths. The male has one very large claw and one small claw. Females have two small claws. All fiddlers live in the intertidal zone.

COLOR: extremely variable.

5. **Pinfish** *(Lagodon rhomboides)*

SIZES: to eight inches.

RANGE: Massachusetts, Bermuda, Gulf of Mexico, to Florida Keys and the Yucatan. They are a wide, flat fish, exhibiting a bluegill-like shape. Impressions of a silvery body with gold horizontal stripes and blue overtones.

6. **Finger Mullet** *(Mugil eurema)*. This is the white mullet.

SIZE: to ten inches—two to five inches for imitations.

RANGE: Massachusetts, Bermuda, Gulf of Mexico to Brazil.

COLOR: silvery sides with dark gray back.

7. **Glass Minnows** Thought to be anchovy or sardine spawn.

SIZES: from one-half to one-and-a-half inches long.

Translucent, almost crystal-clear. It's hard to believe, but very large snook, reds, ladyfish, and jacks will feed with real gluttony on these tiny fry, both under lighted docks and bridges at night in summertime, and especially during the infusion of glass minnows up coastal rivers in the fall. This run begins in early November in Florida and lasts till late December. They move upriver seeking warmer water, coinciding with times that snook, trout, redfish, and ladyfish move to escape the cold of the outside bays and beaches. Snook will feed on these minute forage much like brown trout feed on trico spinners, taking many individuals at one gulp.

8. **Striped Mullet** (*Mugil cephalus*)
   SIZE: to thirty inches.
   RANGE: Cape Cod to Brazil and the Gulf of Mexico.
   COLOR: black above, silver sides with black stripes. All gamefish eat mullet and when the fall run is on, tarpon and snook go on feeding binges.

FAVORITE FORAGE OF BACKCOUNTRY TARPON

These are smaller tarpon, from five to sixty pounds, and not the giant fish over a hundred pounds that are usually but not always found outside the beaches and passes. These fish will eat almost everything and key on what is most prevalent and nourishing in these locations. Baitfishermen on Florida's west coast use select white swimming shrimp most of the time. On the east coast, tarpon anglers use more mullet as live bait. On the outside, west coast bait anglers use pinfish, crabs, and threadfin herring.

1. **Shrimp** (see snook forage for description).
2. **Finger Mullet** in backcountry bays and during fall runs along the east coast (see snook forage for description).
3. **Scaled sardine** and **threadfin herring**, which are similar but larger (see snook forage for description).

4. **Pinfish** (see snook forage for description).

5. **Blue crabs and many other crab species** (see snook forage for description).

6. **Grunts** (family *Haemulidae*)
   SIZES: from two to eighteen inches. These are perch-shaped fish found where tarpon are found; adults usually feed at night, as do tarpon.
   RANGE: Maryland, Bermuda, Gulf of Mexico to Brazil. Various colors, depending on species.

7. **Ladyfish** *(Elops saurus)*
   SIZES: to three feet. Best imitations three to six inches. Ladyfish are closely related to tarpon and when hooked fight and jump like tarpon, but are a favorite prey.
   RANGE: Cape Cod to Bermuda, Gulf of Mexico to Brazil; common in bays, lagoons, and mangrove areas.
   COLOR: dark gray above, silvery sides and white belly.

8. **Catfish Gafftop sail** *(Bagre marinus)*
   SIZE: to two feet.
   RANGE: Massachusetts, Gulf of Mexico to Venezuela.

   Hard-head *(Arium felis)*
   SIZE: to 2 feet.
   RANGE: Massachusetts, Florida, Mexico.
   COLOR: gray above, silvery sides.

9. **Marine worms** *(Polychaetes)*, segmented worms
   SIZES: from two to three inches. Two major groups, errant or free-moving, and sedentary or burrowing, and tube dwellers. Errant worms are often carried out of passes from inside bays on strong ebb tides. These worms are among the most important food sources for bottom-feeding gamefish. Local collection is necessary, as thousands of species and colors exist. The Palolo worm hatch is famous in the Florida Keys. Tarpon and other gamesters feed on these any time they are available. The Palolo worm is really the epitoke (last few segments of the worm), which break off the main worm and is full of eggs or sperm. The epitoke is only two to four inches in length. This "hatch" lasts for a few days in the spring in the Florida Keys, where the segments swarm near the surface.
   RANGE: worldwide, 8,000 species.
   COLOR: almost every color imaginable depending on species.

FAVORITE
FORAGE OF REDFISH

These are the bonefish of the 10,000 Islands and north to the entire Gulf Coast, Georgia and the Carolinas. Shrimp and crabs are the preferred food, as reds are bottom feeders. As they grow larger (bulls), they take more baitfish. They can be sight-fished, while tailing, and mudding like bonefish, but are much larger and stronger.

1. **Shrimp** These include commercial swimming shrimp, shore shrimp and grass shrimp, all of which look like shrimp as most people know them (see snook for description of swimming shrimp).

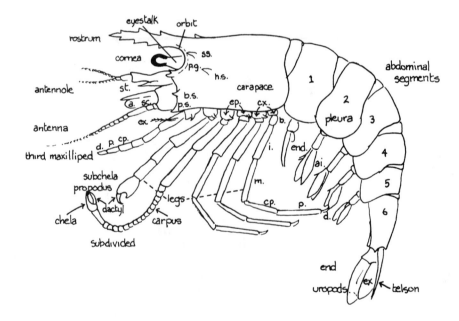

Anatomy of a swimming shrimp

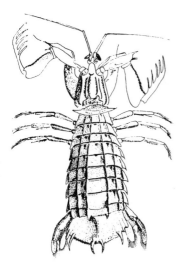

Common mantis shrimp

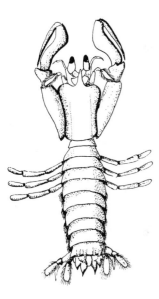

Rock mantis shrimp

2. **Mantis Shrimp** These are not shrimp as we usually think of shrimp. They very closely resemble a praying mantis (the insect) and are heavily fed upon by bonefish, permit, redfish, and other bottom feeders.

Class — *Crustacea*
Order — *Stomatopoda*
Family — *Squillidae*

They burrow in sand, grass flats, and coral crevices. Some lurk near entrance to burrows, others creep up on their prey. There are sixty species on the Atlantic Coast from Cape Cod to Florida, Texas, Mexico, to Brazil and the Bahamas. There are many Pacific species; these are some of the common species.

(a) **Common Mantis** *(Sequilla empusa)*
   SIZE: to eight inches, but one-and-a-half to three inches best for artificial.
   RANGE: Cape Cod to Gulf of Mexico
   COLOR: Variable greenish or bluish green with darker green or blue margins to segments of whitish with yellow to orange body ridge and ground joints of raptorial legs; eyes green

(b) **Rock Mantis** *(Gonodactylus oerstedii)*
   SIZE: to four inches
   RANGE: North Carolina to Brazil and the Bahamas
   COLOR: variable, dark mottled green to black or cream with green mottling

(c) **False Sequilla** *(Pesudosequille ciliate)* or Golden Mantis
   SIZE: to four inches
   RANGE: Southern Florida, Bahamas, to Brazil
   COLOR: Variable, yellowish brown, greenish brown, bright green, pale green, or whitish.

Other common species exhibit colors that range from uniform cream, cream mottled with light gray to olive green, yellowish brown, greenish brown, cream with dark brown bands, and reddish with lighter red markings.
   The color variations between species and even among individuals of the same species mean you should acquire specimens from the area you wish to fish and match those colors. They usually take on the general color of the bottom where they are found.

3. **Snapping Shrimp or Pistol Shrimp** These look like cray fish, but with one greatly enlarged claw. They are widely ranged and are a special favorite of bonefish and redfish.

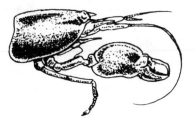

Big-clawed snapping shrimp

They are found in and around their burrows in grass flats, reefs, and oyster bars in both the Atlantic and Pacific. Some common Atlantic species are:

(a) Common or Big-Clawed Snapping Shrimp
(Alpheus heteruchelis)
SIZE: to two inches
RANGE: North Carolina, Brazil, Bahamas
COLOR: Greenish gray

(b) Banded Snapping Shrimp *(A. armillatur)*
SIZE: to two inches
RANGE: same as common snapping shrimp
COLOR: banded with white and greenish tan

(c) Red Snapping Shrimp
SIZE: to two inches
RANGE: same as common snapping shrimp
COLOR: red with white markings

4. Mud Shrimp and Ghost Shrimp These are very similar in appearance to snapping shrimp, except the large claw is not as greatly enlarged. They are also very common in the backcountry and heavily fed upon. They have complex burrows in sand and mud flats. Ghost shrimp prefer clean sand and have larger claws.

Class — *Crustacea*
Order — *Nocopodia*
Family — *Callianasside*

(a) Atlantic Ghost Shrimp or Short-browed Mud Shrimp *(Callinassa atlantica)*
SIZE: to two and a half inches
RANGE: Nova Scotia to Florida
COLOR: white with greenish and yellowish edges and yellow swimmerets

(b) West Indies Ghost Shrimp *(C. major)*
SIZE: to three and three-quarter inches
RANGE: North Carolina to Florida and Louisiana to West Indies to Brazil
COLOR: white or green

(c) Flat-browed Mud Shrimp *(Upogebia affinus)*
SIZE: to four inches
RANGE: Cape Cod to Florida, Texas to Brazil and
West Indies
COLOR: Bluish or yellowish gray, sometimes a
pinkish hue

5. **Crabs** Especially immature blue crabs and mud crabs (see snook)
6. **Scaled Sardines** (see snook for descriptions)
7. **Finger mullet** (see snook for descriptions)

FAVORITE FORAGE OF SPOTTED SEA TROUT

These are fish of the grassy flats. They take topwater and bottom-dwelling food freely.

1. **Shrimp** (see snook and redfish)
2. **Sardines and threadfin herring**
3. **Finger Mullet** (see snook for descriptions)
4. **Glass minnows** (see snook for descriptions)

FAVORITE FORAGE OF BONEFISH

Bonefish, like permit, redfish, and sheepshead, are bottom feeders. They feed on a surprisingly wide variety of aquatic invertebrates found both on outside flats and inside bays and mangrove pools from Florida Bay, Biscayne Bay, many inside areas around Andros and other Bahamian islands, and along the east coast of the Yucatan Peninsula from Ascension Bay south to Belize. Included in their diet are (not in order of preference):

Sea Urchins	Marine Worms
Brittle Stars	Frill-Fin Goby
Annelid Worms	Key Worm Eel
Sea Anemones	Gulf Toadfish

(cont'd.)

Seahorses	Mutton Snapper
Snake Eels	Mahogany Snapper
Mud Crabs	Lane Snapper
Green reef Crabs	Swimming Shrimp
Blue Crabs	Gray Snappers
Spider Crabs	Schoolmasters
Grass Shrimp	Dog Snappers
Squid	White Grunts
Snapping Shrimp	Tomtates
Spiny Lobsters	Dusty Cust Eels
Tulip Conch	Mud Shrimp
Snails	Mantis Shrimp
Clams (favorite prey)	

As you can see from this list, it seems bonefish will eat just about everything, especially bottom dwellers. They do eat some fish, usually in tidal pools where they are easy to chase down, but the staples of their diet are marine invertebrates.

Some special favorites of bonefish are a group of crustaceans contained in the orders *Stomatopoda* (mantis shrimp) and *Decapodia* (snapping shrimp). These invertebrates are not shrimp as we usually think of them. The mantis shrimp look like praying mantis. The snapping shrimp resembles a crayfish with one big claw, or in the case of flat-browed mud shrimp, two smaller claws. One bonefish in the Bahamas was found to contain forty snapping shrimp of a particular species.

Bonefish may or may not be selective, but 40 shrimp to the exclusion of anything else sounds like we'd better know what kind of food forms are most numerous on a particular flat.

(See redfish for description of snapping shrimp, mud shrimp, and mantis shrimp.)

Especially common in the Bahamas and the Florida Keys is the green reef crab and a good imitation is a "must" pattern if you are planning a trip to that area.

Green Reef Crab (*Mithrax spinosissimus*)
SIZE: to one inch
RANGE: Florida, Bahamas, West Indies, to Brazil
HABITAT: reefs, grass beds, shallow flats
COLOR: Carapace olive green with darker green raised bumps, claws dark green, legs brown and hairy, underside medium olive green.

FAVORITE FORAGE OF PERMIT

These wily gamefish are not found in great numbers in classic backcountry but some areas do have schools, especially south of Cape Romano in Florida Bay, Biscayne Bay, and areas of the Bahamas and the Yucatan Peninsula.

These are bottom feeders and will often take a fly when it is sitting still or moving very slowly.

FAVORITE FOODS

Crabs

(a) Blue (see snook for descriptions)

(b) Green Reef (see bonefish for descriptions)

(c) Mud (see snook for descriptions)

Shrimp

(a) Snapping (see redfish for description)

(b) Mantis (see redfish for description)

(c) Mud (see snook for description)

Floating schools of permit feed on crabs and shrimp when a strong tidal flow carries them close to the surface. This phenomenon is found where a deeper channel runs between two shallow areas. The usually wary permit are especially easy to hook when you find this situation.

FAVORITE FORAGE OF JACK CREVALLE

Jacks are very common in the Florida backcountry and in the winter months they can save the day after a cold spell when snook and tarpon turn off. They are similar in appearance to permit and fight just as hard. The main differences are range and feeding habits. Permit are found in greatest numbers on open flats around the lower Florida Keys south to Yucatan Peninsula and west to the Bahamas. Many range around artificial reefs farther north. They prefer crabs and, to a lesser degree, shrimp. Jack crevalle are found from outside islands and into the far back bays and river mouths further north. They are not at all particular in their food. Popping bugs, streamers, shrimp, and crabs will all work on jacks. They will become as selective as snook if working a school of a particular forage species, and the same flies we use for snook are effective for jacks.

FORAGE OF
SNOOK AND TARPON
IN THE WINTER

The diet of snook and tarpon is radically changed when cold weather arrives. This is primarily due to the cold-weather migrations of these fish as they search for warmer water. As the first cold fronts arrive, snook, baby tarpon, and even some giant tarpon begin moving from the outside areas into the backcountry. By December, they can be very far back and many miles up coastal rivers. The food chain is different here, so the gamefish must eat what is available. This water ranges from brackish to fully fresh, but there are species of crabs and baitfish that can tolerate and even thrive in this environment. Blue and other species of swimming crabs have this capacity and we have already described them, but the baitfish need to be understood if we are to be successful in cold weather. After all, winter is the time most people visit Florida and we like to escape the frigid north as much as anyone. When we do, we like to be able to catch fish, so we collected specimens of the bait in the areas where we found the fish, tied flies to imitate them, and tested the imitations. The following is a description of the species we found important in the far backcountry.

1. **Sailfin Molly** *(Poecilia latipinna)*
   COLOR: Olive above, white to yellow below, with about five rows of dark brown spots and iridescent yellow flecks on the side. Males have a large

Baby tarpon feeding on sailfin mollies in a lagoon on the Blackwater River in December. This lagoon is fifteen miles in from the open Gulf.

sail-like dorsal fin with an orange edge with black spots on the outer half and black wavy lines on the lower half. Females are more drab, lack the huge sail and the orange. To five inches.

RANGE: Atlantic and Gulf Coast from Cape Fear, North Carolina, to Veracruz, Mexico. Very abundant in Florida.

HABITAT: Ponds, lakes, sloughs, and quiet, sometimes vegetated backwaters and pools of streams, in fresh and brackish water.

REMARKS: This is a popular and colorful aquarium fish. The species is very common in the coastal rivers, ponds, and lakes in southwest Florida. Because it is so colorfully marked, it is difficult to imitate with conventional ties. We use a latex-body technique, similar to the crab tie, except of course for the shape.

2. Striped Mojarra *(Diapterus plumieri)*

COLOR: Body is dark olive above, tannish silvery on the side with a metallic sheen, with a blackish stripe along the center of each scale row except toward the belly. All the fins except the pectoral fins are dusky; pelvic and anal fins sometimes dark orange. To twelve inches.

RANGE: South Carolina and entire Gulf of Mexico to Brazil.

HABITAT: Brackish and coastal fresh waters in limestone and grassy areas.

3. **Sheepshead Minnow** (*Cyprinodon variegatus*)

COLOR: Irregular dark bands along the silvery sides. Breeding males have a brilliant blue nape, orange cheeks and lower body, and lack the dark bands. Size to three inches.

RANGE: Cape Cod to south Florida and northern Gulf of Mexico to the Yucatan.

HABITAT: Common from fresh water to full sea water.

4. **Inland Silverside** (*Menidia beryllina*)

COLOR: Belly is silvery white, sides and top are translucent gray with a brownish dorsal and golden orange reflections around the face. There is a lateral line that glows green, gold, black, silver, or a combination of all four, depending on the angle of light rays striking the side. Size to four inches.

RANGE: Massachusetts to southern Florida and around the Gulf to northeastern Mexico.

HABITAT: Coastal fresh and tidal waters.

REMARKS: A number of other species are present in these waters, including the Reef, Hardhead, Rough, and Tidewater silverside, all of which can be important at times, but they are so similar, one imitation will cover all the species.

5. **Blackchin Tilapia** (*Sarotherodon melanotheron*)

COLOR: Orange or gold-yellow on the back and upper sides, pale blue below. They often have bars on the side. Size to 6 inches.

RANGE: Africa, Florida and the Middle East. This is an exotic aquarium fish from Africa. The species escaped and has now spread to most brackish bays and freshwater streams.

HABITAT: Lower reaches of streams, tolerant of high salinity.

6. **Spotted Tilapia** (*Tilapia mariae*)

COLOR: Silver-gray to dark olive above, light olive to yellow-brown, with six to seven faint dark bars.

RANGE: West-central Africa and Florida, where it is common.

HABITAT: Mud to sand-bottom canals and warm springs.

One other forage species present in the areas where snook and tarpon winter is the striped mullet, which we have already covered, though we cannot emphasize enough the importance of an imitation of this fish. It is our favorite pattern for backcountry tarpon both in summer and winter.

Some other species of winter forage are the familiar bluegill and the largemouth bass. Sometimes very large tarpon will get as far up the Caloosahatchee River as Lake Okeechobee. Here they dine on what freshwater fishermen consider gamefish.

OTHER GAMEFISH FOUND IN THE BACKCOUNTRY AND THEIR FORAGE

These gamesters are mainly targets of opportunity in backcountry. Some are primarily surface feeders. That is, they will not take forage below their own level and feed mainly on baitfish. Some are primarily bottom feeders and feed on crabs, shrimp, clams, and other bottom-dwelling prey.

BOTTOM FEEDERS

Snappers Feed on shrimps and crabs all year. Found in stream channels, potholes, mangrove shorelines.

Sheepshead Feed on shrimp and crabs. Found on shallow flats and around jetties and other structures.

Black Drum Feed on shrimp and crabs, found mainly north of the 10,000 Islands.

SURFACE FEEDERS

Ladyfish Feed on forage fish around passes, grass flats, bridges.

Bluefish Arrive in late fall and winter in Florida. They are found from the first inside bay to the outside beaches. They migrate to northern latitudes in the summer. They feed mainly on forage fish. On the New England coast, they feed on menhaden, Atlantic herring, silversides, butterfish, and sand eels and are around Long Island Sound and Cape Cod from May to October.

Striped bass   From north Florida to Maine. They are migratory in roughly the same seasons as bluefish and feed on the same forage. Although considered surface feeders, stripers will root on the bottom for sand eels and crabs.

Barracuda   are good winter fish on the Florida Keys and flats. They feed mainly on other fish.

King mackerel   are found in heaviest concentration in the spring and fall on the Gulf Coast. They feed on other fish.

Spanish mackerel   are found in fall and spring in the Gulf. They are found in large bays of the backcountry and feed on forage fish.

Cobia   move on shallow outside areas of flats in the spring and fall and feed on other fish.

Shark   are found almost everywhere, with the warm months being best. They feed mainly on other fish.

Pompano   are found fall and winter in the Gulf. They are found in channels and potholes in Florida Bay and south Florida, and sometimes produce great fly fishing on grassy flats in this area. They feed mainly on forage fish.

FAVORITE FORAGE OF OTHER FISH-EATING GAMEFISH

▼ **Half-Beaks** *(Family Exocoetidae)*

Lower jaw elongated

These are very common forage fish for all species of surface-feeding gamefish. They are found from the open ocean to the backcountry bays and up coastal rivers. They all present a slim, silvery appearance with a dark blackish blue or green back and long beaks. Listed are the most common found inshore and backcountry.

1. **Ballyhoo** *(Hemiramphus brasiliensis)*
   SIZE: to sixteen inches
   RANGE: Massachusetts to Gulf of Mexico to Brazil
   HABITAT: Bays and inshore waters
   COLOR: Tip of lower jaw and upper lobe of caudal fin
   orange-red

2. **Half-Beak** *(Hemiramphus unifusciatus)*
   SIZE: to eleven inches
   RANGE: Maine, Bermuda, Gulf of Mexico, to Argentina
   HABITAT: Bays and estuaries
   COLOR: Tip of lower jaw and upper lobe of caudal fin
   yellowish red

Needlefish (both jaws elongated)

1. **Atlantic Needlefish** *(Strongylura marina)*
   SIZE: to twenty-four inches
   RANGE: Maine, Gulf of Mexico, to Brazil
   HABITAT: Coastal waters, bays, estuaries; enters fresh
   water
   COLOR: Caudal fin bluish

2. **Red-fin Needlefish** *(Strongylura notata)*
   SIZE: to twenty-four inches
   RANGE: Bermuda, Florida, and Central America
   HABITAT: Bays and inlets; enters fresh water
   COLOR: Vertical fins reddish or orangish

Some other common forage fish taken by backcountry game-fish from Maine to Florida, the Yucatan and Bahamas: porgies; grunts; all herring family members; snapper; sand perch; snake eels; toadfish; gobies; crust eels; ladyfish; catfish; butterfish; Atlantic silversides; American sand lance.

COLLECTING

All the prey type listed are common food forms, widely spread throughout the Gulf of Mexico, Atlantic Coast of the United States, Central and South America, the Bahamas, and Caribbean Islands. Gamefish may, however, be feeding on forms available in a specific area at a specific season. To discover what your target is eating, where and when you are fishing, it pays huge rewards to collect forage species where you are fishing and match your imitations to the naturals.

Collecting with a cast net

COLLECTING
FISH SPECIES

There are many easy methods for collecting baitfish. Perhaps the simplest is to venture out at night either with your own very bright light or by using lights around bridges, docks, and piers. Just inside passes are an excellent place to start, especially on a strong outgoing or incoming tide. Collection here will quickly tell you exactly what is really available. The bait is usually so attracted to the lights that it is easy to use a cast net or simple dip net to collect everything in the strong current. Even shrimp, crab, and segmented worm species will be seen, sometimes in great numbers.

Daytime is a little more difficult, but the cast net, thrown into a school of baitfish, still will connect. Another method is to

Collecting forage with a dip net

imitate the baitfishermen. They will start a chum line of chopped-up sardines in the current, then use a cast net, dip net, or even small hooks baited with pieces of chum to capture live bait.

INVERTEBRATE FORMS

Shallow-water areas, such as bonefish flats, grass beds, or silt bays can be sampled by snorkeling and just looking. You must be observant, as bottom-dwelling prey is usually camouflaged and hidden—or both—else they would be eaten all too quickly. If the water is shallow enough to wade, and lots of it is, a sieve box (four 2x2's nailed together with an end closed by a screen) can be used. Merely scoop substrata material into the screen and sift with water. The prey will be uncovered for study. For deeper layers of the bottom, a core sample (a large coffee can with one end open) can be pushed into a likely area. The open end is then covered with the blade of a shovel and lifted. With just a little preliminary work, studying the food available in your area will invoke a personal confidence in your fly selection and your presentation.

If you happen to be fishing out of a fishing camp, there is an easy way to collect prey species. Ask the camp manager or your guides if they can get what you want. They almost always will. We recently fished out of the Golden Bonefish Lodge on Cockney Cay, off Turneffe Reef, Belize. Our guides were Fabian and William Johnson, who also are the owners of this new camp. They were extremely helpful. Besides being very nice people, they are known to be the two best guides in Belize. We merely had to mention that we wished to collect a fish or a shrimp and in a little while someone showed up with them; we had more than we really needed. We gave the kids who lived at the camp a cast net and a dip net. Off they went to chase the prey. They were having so much fun catching minnows and shrimp we had trouble getting them to stop.

5

Realistic Patterns

CARL'S SARDINE

▼ **Scaled Sardine** *(Harengula jaguara)*

This fish is a special favorite of snook, although all other gamefish (except bottom feeders) relish them as well. It is a member of the herring family, a number of which are important forage fish. It is found from southern Florida and the Gulf of Mexico to Brazil, and grows to a length of seven inches.

We tie the fly from one-and-a-half to three inches long, which is more representative. It has a deep belly, a flat back and is thin from side to side. Its eyes are large for its body size and positioned close to the dorsal. The pattern we tie has all the above characteristics and also is a close match for the important related species, such as Spanish sardines, Atlantic thread herring, Atlantic menhaden, and redear sardines. The tie is also a method of imitating any forage species with a deep belly and a flatter back. Good references for fish colors and shapes of baitfish are *The Peterson Guides to Atlantic & Pacific Fishes*.

MATERIALS

Hook   1 to 6 Mustad Stainless Steel #34007 or #AC34068; #AC34068 is the new Mustad accupoint with a triangular point. It has much better penetrating qualities.

Thread   Transparent Coats & Clark thread (purchased at fabric stores)

Body   None

Rear Wing   White lambswool and silk 50%/50% mix fibers (from The Weavers Shop, Rockford, MI). This is a very fine white silvery material with lots of action.

Forward Wing   Same as rear wing

Topping   First, gold Fish Fuzz, topped with green Fish Fuzz or similar hair and one piece of bright green Krystal Flash

Side Wing   Two fibers of silver Krystal Flash

Eyes   Large press-on eyes (from Witchcraft Tape Products, Coloma, MI)

Cement   Five-minute epoxy on eye and head only

TYING STEPS

1. Place hook in vise and wind on clear mono thread. Cement base with thinned E-6000 or nail polish.
2. Tie in bunch of white lambswool and silk mix to bend of the hook.
3. Tie in several bunches of white lambswool and silk mix at bend of hook on the underside, ahead of the barb towards the eye. You are forming a deeper belly than dorsal of the fly to look like a Matuka or Aztec except the fibers are on the ventral, not the dorsal. These fibers should not go much beyond the point or they will foul when cast.
4. Tie in one slim bunch of gold Fish Fuzz on the top of the hook to extend back to the tail, then a slimmer bunch of bright green Fish Fuzz on top of the gold.
5. Tie in two strands of silvery iridescent Krystal Flash along both sides; wing and tie off head; add one piece of bright green in the middle of the back. This represents an

electric-green streak that shows up when light hits the dorsal directly.

 Press on the eyes on each side of the head, close to the top of the head. These eyes have an adhesive on the back so they stay in place.

7 Place five-minute epoxy on the eyes and head only. This is for durability. Do not allow the epoxy to get into the hair except to hold on eyes.

CARL'S CRABS

▼ **Common Blue Crab** *(Callinectes sapidus)*

Permit love blue crabs, but a large number of other gamefish will certainly not turn them down. Blue crabs range from Cape Cod to Uruguay and are especially common in estuaries, where they range into fresh water. Blue crabs and a number of relative species have hind legs which have adapted to swimming paddles and are capable of rapid movement. We will explain the tying steps of blue crabs, but the same instruction can be used for any number of species, many of which are very important to other gamefish. For instance, small wharf crabs and mud crabs are extremely common in southwest Florida, and the snook and redfish love them. Bonefish love the green reef crabs of the Florida Keys and the Bahamas, so don't limit yourself to one species of crabs. There are at least seventeen species which we have found useful in the backcountry. With this tie and a little modification of shape and color you can produce a very realistic imitation for any species in the world.

MATERIALS

Hook #1 to #8 Mustad Stainless Steel #34007 or #AC34068

Thread White 3/0 mono cord or Kevlar

Body White egg fly yarn

Legs and Underside Rub-R-Mold (flexible mold compound—pure liquid latex) from a craft shop

Eyes Burnt mono twenty- to eighty-pound test, depending on size required

Feelers Cream boar's bristles

Coloring Sharpie waterproof pens (from art store) or Pantone pens (better shades but not as permanent)

TYING STEPS

❶ First draw or trace the outline of the crab's underside, legs, claws, and swimming flippers on a piece of paper. You can run your initial drawing through a copy machine and produce any number you wish for future use. You can also reduce or enlarge on some machines. Then fill a Monojet Irrigation Syringe with liquid latex. (Syringe can be obtained from your local friendly dentist. It is disposable and inexpensive.)

❷ Lay down with syringe a layer of liquid latex on tracing or drawing paper and let set up for one hour. Then inject a second layer for bulk, as it will shrink while hardening. Sometimes three layers are necessary. Let cure for seventy-two hours at 70° Fahrenheit. (Warmer temperature cures faster—cooler temperature cures slower).

❸ Place hook in vise and wrap a firm foundation and cement with E-6000 or nail polish.

❹ Spin white egg yarn on either the top or bottom of hook, depending on whether you want the hook to ride up or down. Spin in the same manner as when constructing a muddler head. The yarn should be as long as the crab is wide.

❺ When hook is full of yarn, tie off head and cement with thinned E-6000 or nail polish.

❻ Clip the yarn in the shape of the crab's body. In the case of a blue crab, it is twice as wide as long. Most tiers shape the body so the head of the crab is on the side. This is because most crabs *crawl* sideways. Blue crabs and other species of swimming crabs *swim* (very fast) in any direction they wish including backwards, so you may tie the head to the front or side and it will still imitate nature.

❼ Peel latex legs and belly from drawing paper, place on underside of yarn body and cement with liquid latex. Cut a few lead strips to shape of tail (or flattened split shot) and place on underside and cover with latex.

⑧ Let the latex set up for one hour. Then with syringe, place the anatomy of the tail and thoracic segments on belly. Let this set up one hour.

⑨ Make eyes from nylon leader material by burning tips. Insert into yarn at head and cement with a five-minute epoxy.

⑩ Clip two short segments from boar's bristles and insert in yarn just inside eyes and cement with thinned five-minute epoxy. This step is optional; it may be overkill in exact imitation, especially on very small bonefish patterns.

⑪ Spray yarn with Scotchgard to waterproof the yarn. If this step is not taken, the fly sometimes will not turn over if it lands upside down, unless a gross amount of lead is used. The use of a waterproofing agent will allow you to use much less weight than other crab patterns. It is then much easier to cast, and turns over beautifully in the water.

⑫ The last step is to color the crab whatever shade is needed for the species you are tying. I use Sharpie waterproof permanent ink pens or Pantone pens with the wide points. It is very helpful to have a color photograph of the species you are tying. Most crabs have a variety of tones and colors, and vary greatly even in the same species. Without a picture to refer to, you cannot be accurate. You can get good color guides from various books such as *Field Guide to North American Sea Shore Creatures* and *Peterson Field Guide — Southern & Caribbean Seashore*. (For other field guides for the Pacific Coast and other countries, see bibliography.) Some species, such as wharf crabs, are small as adults. On larger species, such as the blue crabs, you are not imitating adult crabs, but very immatures. These are very different in color, usually lighter. No good photographs exist for immatures that we know of, so we collect them alive, place them in a photographic aquarium and get a good color print that we use for reference.

COMMENTS ON CRAB TYING

I know the above pattern looks like a very intricate tie, but it really is quite easy once you have tied a few. Much of the tying time is just waiting for the latex to cure. The actual tying time is only about thirty to forty-five minutes. The pattern is effective enough to warrant the time involved. If maximum production is desired, a mold for the legs, claws and underbody can be made with vinyl Polysiloxane Impression Material by Kerr. (Can be obtained from your local dentist.) You can mix a few drops of translucent acrylic paint into the liquid latex and the color will be inside the finished legs and belly, impossible to wear off. When finished, paint some Armor-All on legs to keep them supple. The yarn comes in many colors. If you wish to tie a species with a solid color, such as a green reef crab, it is easier to use green from the start.

If you are using the crab for permit you need to have patterns with varying sink rates, slow and fast.

SWIMMING SHRIMP

▼ **White Commercial Swimming Shrimp** *(Penaeus setiferus)*

Although every species of gamefish in the backcountry eats shrimp, baby tarpon up to fifty pounds are especially partial to these decapods. The three- to four-inch size select white is the favorite live bait of the local anglers in the Marco Island, Everglade City, Chokoloskee areas. Bonefish and redfish immatures prefer smaller species such as snapping shrimp, grass shrimp, mantis and false mantis shrimp, and shore shrimp. Other species of southern commercial shrimp, such as the pink shrimp (*P. duorarum*) and the brown shrimp (*P. aztecus*) are very similar to the white shrimp. The shade of colors implied by the numbers are misleading, especially in immatures. The following pattern is for all of the above with some minor color and size changes. All of these species are widespread. The adults lay eggs offshore and the young drift in on incoming tides to mature in the inshore grassy bays where snook, reds, bonefish, and baby tarpon feed. At maturity, they migrate to the open Gulf with strong outgoing tides. During such migrations, gamefish go on selective feeding binges. This same tie can be used for any species of swimming shrimp worldwide.

MATERIALS

Hook Mustad Stainless Steel 3XL size #1/0 to #8. For the smaller-mouthed bonefish, use #6–8 Mustad #AC34068 (accupoint).

Thread White mono

Body (Carapace and abdomen) Large species: Polar Bear or Spectra Streamer Hair (Polar Bear colors) by Umpqua. Smaller species: Fish Hair or Fish Fuzz or lambswool.

Belly White mohair yarn

Front Legs (Maxillipods) Same as body

Swimming Legs (Pleopods) White hen hackle

Antenna White boar's bristles

Eyes Burnt mono

Carapace Clipped cock hackle segment

Tail Same as body

TYING STEPS

This pattern is tied to swim backward. If you want it to swim forward, just reverse the ends. The naturals usually swim forward slowly, then go backward when startled. We have had great success with this tied both ways.

1. Place hook in vise and wrap a firm foundation. Cement with thinned E-6000 or nail polish.
2. Tie in a small bunch of Spectra Hair, or Fish Fuzz, etc., on underside of hook for maxillipods.
3. Tie in a slightly shorter bunch of same hair on top of hook for antennule and antennal scale.
4. Tie in boar's bristle antenna.
5. Take some white mohair yarn and wrap a ball one-quarter the length of the hook from the bend toward the eye. This represents the ventral of the carapace.
6. Tie in burnt mono eyes.
7. Tie in light gray or tan clipped hackle stem behind ball of yarn on top of hook to imitate the rostrum.

Close-up of the head showing
antenial scale

⑧ Tie in two small bunches of Spectra Hair, or Fish Fuzz, etc., a little short of the shrimp's eyes, on top and sides of hook to simulate the white top of the carapace.

⑨ Tie in a light olive or tan marabou fiber and one hen hackle feather behind ball of yarn and take tying thread to hook eye. The hen hackle should be tied in at the base of the hackle with the long fluff fiber intact.

⑩ Wrap the olive or tan marabou to eye and tie off. This gives the fly a slightly olive tint which shows through the Spectra Hair. If you want a tan tint, use tan marabou.

⑪ Wrap the white hen hackle to eye and tie off. These represent the pleopods or swimming legs.

⑫ Tie in some Spectra Hair or Fish Fuzz, etc., on top and sides of the hook so the fibers extend just to the beginning of the carapace where the fur bunch begins. Leave a few fibers extending beyond the eye for the tail.

⑬ Tie off the head and clip any Spectra fibers which are too long or too bushy.

⑭ Optional — At this point, I used to coat the top of the fly with clear worm plastic or thinned E-6000. The worm plastic gives a very soft feel to the pattern. The E-6000 achieves a firm but resilient imitation. I found the more perfectly I shaped the Spectra in the first place, the less coating I needed and the easier it was to apply. After I tied a dozen flies, I looked at the uncoated fly and decided it looked fine without adding any plastic and found it was lighter and easier to cast. I now tie the pattern without any coating, but some people like the looks of the coating, so take your pick. If desired, the finished fly can be tinted with marking pens to imitate the subtle tan spots of the naturals.

COMMENTS ON SWIMMING SHRIMP, SNAPPING SHRIMP, MUD SHRIMP, MANTIS SHRIMP, COMMON SHORE SHRIMP

The tie for the other types of shrimp are very similar to Swimming Shrimp with slight variations in shape. For instance, Snapping Shrimp are more robust and the body needs to be shaped that way. Mantis Shrimp are longer and more slender. Snapping Shrimp have one large claw (like a lobster) and one small claw on the other side. These we fabricate out of liquid latex and tie in at the bend of the hook. Mantis Shrimp have two front legs, which make it look like a praying mantis. We make these out of liquid latex also. You can substitute hackle tips for simplicity.

When you are tying any of these patterns, it really helps if you have a good picture of the natural. If you don't have your own, you can get field guides (*The Peterson Field Guide to Atlantic Seashore* by Ken L. Gosner, *The Audubon Society Field Guide to North American Seashore Creatures* and others), which will give you sizes and colors of the most common species.

S & R
WHITE MULLET
(Mugil Curema)

This fly pattern is one of our favorite all-around searching flies. Mullet are a staple of small and large tarpon and this fly is deadly on snook, tarpon, larger redfish, and many other gamefish, including shark and barracuda. Finger mullet are young mullet, three to five inches or so, and are present all year long in the backcountry. This pattern imitates the white mullet, which is the most abundant mullet in tropical America. It is found from Massachusetts to Brazil. This fish is long, fairly robust, with a round body, and has eyes placed in the middle of its head that are large for its size. The shape is very different from the scaled sardine. Our original pattern was pure white with no embellishments. It was so effective that we were not sure we could improve on it, but we think we have.

MATERIALS

Hook   1/0 to 2 Mustad Stainless Steel #34007 or #AC34068 (accupoint)

Thread   Coats & Clark Transparent Thread

Rear Wing   White lambswool fibers

Body   White mohair yarn

Front Wings   White lambswool fibers and a few strands of pearlescent Flashabou or Krystal Flash

Topping   Medium gray Fish Fuzz

Gills   Bright pink mohair strands

Eyes   Large press-on eyes

TYING STEPS

1. Place hook in vise and wind on transparent thread.
2. Tie a bunch of white lambswool at bend of hook the same length as hook shank.
3. Take a few strands of mohair yarn and wrap body to the head. You must comb out the strands as you are wrapping so they don't get trapped under the next wrap. You should end up with little fibers sticking out all around the body, much like a hackled palmered fly. This produces the round body of the natural.
4. Tie in a bunch of white lambswool for the forward wing and top with medium gray Fish Fuzz.
5. Tie in some bright pink mohair for gills, and finish head.
6. Press on the eyes and coat the eyes and head with five-minute epoxy.

S & R BAY
ANCHOVIES

(Anchoa mitchilli)

This tiny species is a favorite of snook, jack crevalle, and lady-fish, especially at night under lights on bridges and around docks. These very small, round, slim, silvery fish are carried in and out of the passes by powerful spring tides and are irresistibly attracted to snook lights on docks and bridge lights. The gamefish will engage in feeding orgies under these lights and they can become quite selective.

Bay anchovies grow as large as four inches, but our pattern is usually three-quarters of an inch long. Their range is from Maine to Florida, and the entire Gulf of Mexico to Yucatan. They are found mostly in shallow bays and estuaries, are common in brackish water, but are found to depths of 120 feet as well. Our pattern is also a good simulation of a number of other species of anchovies also common to the backcountry everywhere.

MATERIALS

Hook   Mustad #34007 Stainless Steel 6–8 or #AC34068 (accupoint)

Thread   Coats & Clark Transparent Thread

Rear Wing   A few fibers of white lambswool and silk mix

Body   None

Front Wing   A few fibers of white lambswool and silk mix topped by a few fibers of gold Fish Fuzz

Side Band   One piece of silver Flashabou

Eyes   Press-on eyes in middle of head

TYING STEPS

❶   Place hook in vise and wrap on thread base and coat with thinned E-6000.

2. Tie in rear wing of lambswool/silk mix fibers at bend of hook. Use much fewer fibers than for mullet as these are slim naturals.

3. Tie in a small bunch of silk lambswool mix fibers for front wing on top and bottom of hook. This is topped with a very few fibers of gold Fish Fuzz.

4. Tie in one piece of silvery or pearlescent Flashabou on each side right on the lateral line. This represents the flat silver band on the sides of the naturals.

5. Press on eyes in middle of head. Tie off head; cement with five-minute epoxy.

CARL'S
SWIM-AWAY FLIES

These are flies which, when cast on a slack leader, will dive down and "swim" away in the opposite direction of the caster. They are not exact imitations, but can be shaped to suggest shrimp, crabs, and minnows. Some people will call them lures, not flies, but they are hand-tied. They are light, so they can be easily cast with a fly rod; they are resilient, so fish will not instantly eject the pattern; and they are tied with normal fly materials. We got the idea for these flies from a bass plug which is sold on TV called "Flying Lure." For us, the idea filled the need to get under the mangrove trees at higher tide levels. Snook and other gamefish feed in the roots of the trees at these times and often will not come out. These flies go in after them. They will also go after trout under logs or brush, and bass under docks.

SWIM-AWAY FLY—
SHRIMP PATTERN

MATERIALS

Hook Stainless Steel 4XL saltwater hooks or Mustad #AC3468 (accupoint). You need a hook that is fairly light. The heavier the hook, the more lead is needed for balance.

Thread 3/0 monocord

Body   Mylar tape (Witchcraft Tape Products, Coloma, MI) This comes in hundreds of colors and styles and has an adhesive back. Any flat material can be used; soft plastic sheets or even a piece of rubber cut from an old inner tube.

Eyes   Artificial flower stamen or burnt mono

Underbody   Flat lead strip (wrap-around ribbon sinkers by Worth from live bait shop)

Tuning Lead   Wide lead tape from Orvis

Antenna and Front Legs   White fish hair or Fish Fuzz or any hair you like. (For bass patterns we often use Sili Legs.)

TYING STEPS

1. Place hook in vise and wrap thread to form a firm underbody.
2. Tie in a flat strip of lead on top of hook three-quarters of the length of the hook shank and extending beyond the first part of the bend to just beyond bend. The last part of the lead is not tied to the hook, but extends straight and is freestanding.
3. Cut a piece of mylar tape to the desired shape. In this case, cut it long with rounded ends.
4. Peel off the paper on the back of the mylar tape and press sticky side to the flat lead so it is straight, level, and even on both sides.
5. Cement on with thinned E-6000.
6. Tie in eyes at head of hook.
7. Tie in white hair at eye to extend away from the hook point.
8. Tune the fly with Orvis lead tape.
9. Cover mylar with E-6000 or liquid latex and color with permanent marking pens as desired (Shrimp pattern — white or silver with small tan spots).

COMMENTS ON TUNING SWIM-AWAY FLIES

The balance of these flies is critical. Correctly tuned patterns swim best on 3X or six- to eight-pound-test leader. This is fine for bass, but a five-pound snook will destroy an eight-pound-test leader. If the flies are perfectly tuned and manipulated, you can use thirty-pound test, which is adequate for most back-country gamefish. We have tested these patterns against the commercial bass "Flying Lure" and they swim at least three times farther in shallow water because they are lighter and can be tuned.

Of the first three dozen flies we tied, three sank like a rock, but most would swim six to eight inches away for every one foot of water depth. Five would swim twelve inches or more for every one foot of water depth. We found it's better to underweight them and add lead later for perfect tuning.

To tune, we fill a bathtub and place a fly on the surface. The fly is released and the distance it travels is observed. The flies should be heavier at the bend of the hook so they dive at about a 25° to 35° angle. If it sinks level, add lead to the body or wing at the bend of the hook. If it dives at more than a 45° angle, add lead just behind the eye. If the fly swims well but goes to the right or left, bend the wing right or left as needed. Once you have it tuned, carefully cover with E-6000 or liquid latex. When this dries, the shape cannot be easily altered, except perhaps by a barracuda!

NEEDLEFISH AND HALF-BEAKS

Probably every fish-eating gamester in the ocean eats these common forage fish. Most are so similar in appearance, one generalized pattern is very close for the four specific species detailed in Chapter 5 and can be used as a good general forage-fish pattern. They are especially effective around mangrove roots and shallow bays surrounded by mangroves.

MATERIALS

Hook   1/0 to 8 Mustad Stainless #34007 or #AC34068

Thread   Transparent Coats & Clark

Body   none

Wing   White Fish Fuzz or polar bear or lambswool or half lambswool and silk mix under blue Fish Fuzz under dark gray Fish Fuzz

Side Wings   Two fibers of Flashabou

Eyes   Press-on eyes

TYING STEPS

1. Place hook in vise and wind on mono thread; cement with E-6000.
2. Tie in white Fish Fuzz, etc., at bend of hook.
3. Tie in a thin layer of dark blue and dark gray over white.
4. Tie in two fibers of Flashabou, etc., on each side of Fish Fuzz.
5. Wrap clear thread to eye to form a long beak.
6. Press on eyes and cement with five-minute epoxy.

   (a) Fish Fuzz is finer than polar bear, but has the same shiny translucence and a lot more action.

   (b) Lambswool is superfine, but not shiny or translucent and has the most action of all.

   (c) Lambswool-silk mix is superfine and the silk adds flash and has very good action. This is the best for very small flies, sizes 4, 6, 8.

CARL'S IMITATOR (PINFISH)

This is a method of tying any wide-bodied forage fish with a bass or bluegill shape. It will work with other species such as grunts, porgies, tilapia, snappers, sandperch, etc. The colors and shapes must be modified for various species. If one lives on the west coast of the United States, New Zealand, or anywhere else, you can obtain a guide (listed in the bibliography) for your area and imitate your particular local species with this shape.

MATERIALS

Hook   4/0 to 6 Mustad Stainless #34007 or #AC34068

Thread   Transparent Coats & Clark

Tail   Gray hen hackle feather clipped to shape of fish's tail fin and fastened to a length of twenty-pound-test mono

Body   Behind hook—Iridescent fly braid piping, same as the ground color of the natural

Body   On hook—one Spectra Hair

Wing   Fish Hair, Fish Fuzz, lambswool

Gill   Red Fish Fuzz

Eye   Press-on eye

TYING STEPS

❶   Place hook in vise and wind on clear mono; cement base with thinned E-6000 or nail polish.

❷   Cut a section of gray hen hackle tip to the shape of a fish's tail fin and secure to a piece of straight twenty-pound-test mono.

❸   Run mono through the braid piping and secure both to hook bend.

❹   Tie a couple of half-hitches around tail end of piping to close end; cement.

❺   Tie in a bunch of light blue Fish Hair or spectrahair at bend of hook on top and bottom of piping so they slope back on top and under the piping.

❻   Tie alternate sections of light yellow and light blue on top and bottom of hook until head is reached.

❼   Tie in three pieces of Flashabou on either side of wing.

❽   Tie in red Fish Fuzz for gills.

❾   Press on eyes to the dorsal of head and cement with five-minute epoxy.

NOTE: The three different wing materials each give a different effect. The spectrahair is stiff but gives a very translucent, almost bioluminescent effect. The lambswool is opaque but has a very wiggly action in water. The Fish Fuzz is halfway in between these two effects.

CARL'S SHRIMPY

This deadly impressionistic pattern breathes when retrieved and can be tied in various sizes and colors to simulate many species of shrimp. We tie it in five color phases: brown shrimpy, cream shrimpy, olive shrimpy, pink shrimpy, and yellowish shrimpy. These will cover just about every species you may encounter anywhere in the world. In the Florida backcountry, we start fishing with brown or cream. In the Bahamas, the yellow or olive are often better. The pink version is best around live coral. The tan works well in the Florida Keys.

MATERIALS

Hook   #1 to 8 Mustad Stainless Steel #34007 or #AC34068

Thread   White 3/0 monocord

Body   Cream or tan or olive mohair yarn

Tail   Hackle feathers

(a) brown shrimpy: grizzly inside, light brown badger middle, tannish cree on outside

(b) cream shrimpy: light grizzly inside, tannish badger middle, light creamish cree outside

(c) olive shrimpy: dyed olive grizzly inside, dyed light olive badger middle, dyed light olive cree outside

(d) yellow shrimpy: dyed light yellowish grizzly inside, dyed yellow badger middle, dyed light yellow cree outside

(e) pink shrimpy: grizzly inside, dyed reddish badger middle, light dyed pink cree outside

Eyes   Burnt mono

Hackle   Same as tail, all wrapped together

TYING STEPS

1 Place hook in vise and wind on thread; cement with E-6000.

2. Tie in tailfeathers—three on each side so they "V" out on each side.
3. Tie in burnt mono eyes so they are a little beyond bend of hook.
4. Tie in hackle and wrap at bend of hook.
5. Tie in mohair body, brushing out yarn so some fibers protrude from the side.
6. Tie off and cement head with five-minute epoxy.

These can be tied weighted or unweighted and so they ride right side up or upside down. In backcountry bays we find we do not need weight or weedless flies, but in deep cuts with tide running or on cuts between flats we use some weight (lead wrapped around hook shank before body is wrapped). On the flats in Florida Keys and the Bahamas we tie them to ride upside down both weighted and unweighted.

DEADLY EEL

This pattern has wonderful undulating action when retrieved. It is incredibly easy to tie and is one of the best searching flies we know of. It could imitate any of the hundreds of species of marine worms, eels, or very long, thin fish species.

MATERIALS

Hook   1–6 Mustad Stainless Steel #34007 or #AC34068

Thread   White 3/0 monocord

Tail   White lambswool

Body   White mohair yarn

Side strips   Two only, pearlescent Flashabou

TYING STEPS

1. Place hook in vise and wrap thread; cement with E-6000.
2. Tie a bunch of white lambswool at bend of hook about the same length as the hook shank.
3. Wrap the white mohair yarn for body, combing it out with a toothbrush so fibers protrude from sides.

Tie in two pieces of pearlescent Flashabou on each side.

5 Tie off head and cement with five-minute epoxy.

This pattern can be tied in any color; green, pink, and orange are very effective at certain times.

SEA DEVIL

If we were forced to use only one pattern in the salt, it would definitely be the Sea Devil. It not only has a great silhouette and tremendous action in the water, but, if tied properly, is the most tangle-free fly we've ever used in the backcountry. The key to its non-fouling ability is the way the tail is formed. It must be tied so that the first few fibers, the lowest ones, are extremely short, only one-quarter-inch or so. Then each succeeding fiber must be slightly longer than the last one. In this manner, each strand protects the next one above it from fouling. We try to create this taper as best as possible during the tying process by laying in numerous hair clumps of varying lengths; however, after the fly is tied, we give the tail a final trim with a pair of scissors.

The original Sea Devil was all white. But now we tie it in a variety of colors with pink-and-white being the most popular. Yellow-and-white and chartreuse-and-white are also deadly. We tie them as large as 3/0 and down to size 2 and even smaller; however, 1/0's are what we use the most.

MATERIALS

Hook   Mustad #3407 or equivalent, size 2/0-2, 1/0 most common

Thread   White 3/0 monocord

Body   White Mohlon yarn

Tail   White Tasmanian Devil or equivalent. Lambswool can be substituted. Two strands of pearl Krystal Flash on each side.

Wing   White Tasmanian Devil, equivalent, or lambswool. Two strands of pearl Krystal Flash on each side.

❶ Place hook in vise, add lead wire if desired, wrap thread and cement. We usually weight with twelve to fifteen turns of .020 wire.

❷ Tie in clumps of Tasmanian Devil to form a tapered tail, starting low with very short fibers and progressing upwards to the longest fibers, which should be one-and-a-quarter to one-and-a-half times the body length.

❸ Tie in two pearl Krystal Flash strands on each side of the tail.

❹ Tie in mohlon yarn in front of tail and make one wrap. Spiral thread to eye of hook.

❺ Tie in a *small* clump of Tasmanian Devil fibers on top of shank with mohlon yarn. Take two more wraps in front of clump. Continue this procedure to eye creating a Matuka- or Aztec-style wing. Keep the yarn in your right hand so you can maintain heavy tension during the entire wing-mounting process.

❻ Secure yarn with tying thread and cut off excess.

❼ Tie in two pearl Krystal Flash strands on each side of wing.

❽ Tie off head and cement.

❾ Trim tail on a bias to ensure nonfouling feature.

To make the pink-and-white version, use pink Tasmanian Devil for the wing and upper half of the tail. Other popular colors are yellow-and-white, chartreuse-and-white, all yellow and all black. All white Devils can be marked up with permanent markers to match specific minnows and baitfish. Mylar and other flashy type yarns can be substituted for the mohlon to create unique effects.

DON PHILLIPS'S
BABY MULLET

This is a pattern developed by Don Phillips (originator of the boron fly rod). It is an excellent finger-mullet imitation and has a terrific darting, erratic action.

MATERIALS

Hook   1/0 stainless-steel 2x-long, Mustad #34011

Thread   3/0 white monocord

Wing   Six white saddle hackles tied on the hook shank for three-fourths of an inch, extending two inches beyond the bend
Ten to fifteen strands of pearl Krystal Flash tied over the saddle hackles; then, two bunches of white Marabou at the bend

Body   White deepwater chenille wound over the wing base

Head   Spun light deer hair clipped to five-eighths-inch diameter and half-inch long

Eyes   4mm doll eyes

TYING STEPS

1. Place hook in vise, wind thread; cement.
2. Tie in saddle hackles.
3. Tie in Krystal Flash over saddle hackles.
4. Tie in Marabou at hook bend.
5. Wrap white chenille over wing's base.
6. Spin light deer hair and clip to shape.
7. Attach eyes with Zap-A-Gap and color top of fly with a black stripe using a Pantone pen.

CARL'S SIMPLE SHRIMP

This is a very easy shrimp pattern to tie, but it is effective and has a realistic appearance. The hair has a wavy motion when retrieved, along with a translucent look. It can be tied in sizes from 4/0 to 8 and the colors can be varied for different species of the natural you are imitating.

MATERIALS

Hook   4/0 to 8 Mustad #AC34068

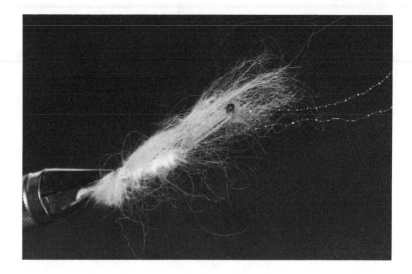

Simple shrimp

Thread White 3/0 Dynacord

Tail White lambswool and tan lambswool

Body White mohair

Wing Same as tail

Eye Burnt mono

TYING STEPS

1. Place hook in vise and wrap thread; cement.
2. Tie in a bunch of white lambswool at the bend of the hook, a little longer than the hook shank.
3. Tie in some tan fibers on top and sides of white hair.
4. Tie in a piece of tan mohair yarn over top.
5. Tie in eyes of burnt mono.
6. Wrap body of white mohair.
7. Tie in some white lambswool to slope over body to eyes.
8. Tie in some tan mohair fibers over white hair on top and sides.
9. Tie off head; cement.

The lambswool has a very fine grain; the mohair is slightly more coarse. This combination gives a textured effect that produces a realistic imitation. The pink version is the best fly we have ever fished for bonefish in the Bahamas.

ATLANTIC SILVERSIDES

(Menidia menidia)

This species is a favorite of stripers, bluefish, bonito, and little tunny. Its range is from the Gulf of St. Lawrence to northeastern Florida, and it is found along beaches and mouths of inlets and coastal streams. It grows to six inches and swarms in huge numbers. The coasts of Martha's Vineyard and Long Island Sound have large schools of silversides and stripers, and other gamefish herd them inshore and gorge on them, along with sand eels (American sand lance), which live in the same area. These are slim, silvery fish with a bright stripe down the midline and a darker dorsal.

The reef silversides is a dynamite imitation for bonefish, snappers, jacks, and just about anything that lives around a reef. The same imitation can be used since the naturals are very similar. We tie it in three color phases. The top half can be gray, tan, or olive green; the rest is the same.

MATERIALS

Thread   Transparent Coats & Clark

Body   Pearlescent hollow Ever-Glow

Rear Wing   Light gray Fish Fuzz

Forward Underwing   White silk brick over white Fish Fuzz

Forward Top Wing   Tan long Fish Hair or Fish Fuzz, under dark brown Fish Fuzz

Side Stripe   Silver Flashabou, one strand of green Krystal Flash

Eyes   Press-on eyes

Cement   Five-minute epoxy on head and eyes only

TYING STEPS

❶   Tie in gray rear wing at bend of hook.
❷   Tie in Larvilace at bend and wrap to head.

❸ First tie in a bunch of white Fish Fuzz under the head and then a bunch of silk brick on either side of the Fish Fuzz.

❹ Tie in a slim bunch of tan Big Fly Hair, then a slimmer bunch of brown Fish Fuzz over the head.

❺ Tie in one strip of silver mylar on each side of the midline, and one strip of green Krystal Flash.

❻ Place eyes, and cement head and eyes.

This same tie can be used to imitate sand lance by tying an even slimmer fly and varying the colors. Sand lance are silver on the lower half of the body and olive green on the top half, with a bright yellow-green glowing line on the midline.

TABLES OF NATURALS

The following tables describe various prey forms common to backcountry and flats of North America, Central America and South America, plus the Bahamas, with descriptions and habitat. All the forms provide food for various gamefish in this region. The fly tier should find the section useful when imitating species in his location.

FISH

SPECIES	DESCRIPTION	SIZE	HABITAT	RANGE
Bay Anchovy (*Anchoa mitchilli*) 150 species	slender silvery body with flat silver strips at midline	to 4″; juveniles 3/4″	shallow bays and estuaries, common in brackish water; very abundant in tropical waters	Gulf of Maine to Florida, entire Gulf of Mexico to Yucatan
Sea Catfish Gafftopsail (*Bagre marinus*)	bluish above, silvery below, very large dorsal fin	to 2′; juveniles 3″–6″	shallow water; enters brackish water	Massachusetts, Gulf of Mexico to Venezuela

(cont'd.)

FISH

SPECIES	DESCRIPTION	SIZE	HABITAT	RANGE
Hardhead (*Arius Felis*)	brownish above, white below	to 2'; juveniles 3"–6"	same as above	Massachusetts, Gulf of Mexico, Florida and Mexico
Cust Eels Dusty Cust Eel (*Parophidon schmidti*) 12 species this region	dusky brown, looks like short eel	to 4"; juveniles to 2"	shallow coastal waters, especially turtle grass beds	Bermuda, Florida, Bahamas to northern South America
Gobies Frill-Finned Gobi (*Bathygobias soporator*) 17 species this region	shades of brown, five dark horizontal stripes; closely resembles sculpins	to 3"	rocky tide pools	Bermuda, Florida, Gulf of Mexico to Brazil
Grunts Barred (*Conodon nobilis*)	various shapes, mostly like smallmouth bass, tan with brown bars	to 1'; juveniles 2"–3"	bays	Eastern Florida, Texas, Jamaica to Brazil
Pigfish (*Orthopristis chrysoptera*)	gray with bluish cast and yellow spots	to 15"; juveniles 2"–3"	bays and coastal waters	New York, Bermuda to Florida and Mexico
Porkfish (*Anisotremus virginicus*)	two black sloping bars on head, body blue-and-yellow, stripes above, white with yellow stripes below	to 15"; juveniles 2"–3"	bays and coastal waters	Bermuda, Bahamas, Yucatan to Brazil
White Grunt (*Haemulon plumieri*) 12 other species this region, all common and widespread	bluish white with many alternating blue-and-yellow lines on head, few on body	to 18"; juveniles 2"–3"	bays and coastal waters	Maryland, Bermuda, Gulf of Mexico to Brazil

(cont'd.)

SPECIES	DESCRIPTION	SIZE	HABITAT	RANGE
Needlefish Seven species this region, both jaws elongated. **Atlantic Needlefish** (*Strongylura marina*)	very slim, silvery with green backs, caudal fin bluish	to 2′; juveniles 2″–6″	open ocean to backcountry bays and up coastal bays	Massachusetts to Gulf of Mexico to Brazil and Caribbean
Redfin Needlefish (*Strongylura notata*)	same as Atlantic Needlefish, but dorsal, caudal, and fins reddish or orangish	to 2′; juveniles 2″–6″	Coastal, in bays and inlets, enters fresh waters	Bermuda, Florida, Bahamas to Lesser Antilles and Central America
Halfbeaks Five species in this region. Lower jaw elongated. **Ballyhoo** (*Heriramphus braziliensis*)	slim but not quite as slim as needle-fish; same general color, tip of lower jaw longer than upper, back bluish black, lobe of caudal fin orange red	to 16″; juveniles 2″–6″	common in shore waters, bays and near reefs	New York and Gulf of Mexico to Brazil. Replaced in Bermuda by similar species
Halfbeak (*Hemiramphus unifusciatus*)	same general color as needle-fish but tip of lower jaw and upper lobe of caudal fin yellow-ish red	to 11″; juveniles 2″–4″	bays and estuaries	Maine, Bermuda, Gulf of Mexico to Argentina
Herring 17 species **Atlantic Menhaden** (*Brevoortia tyranrus*) also known as moss bunker, porgy, fatback; four species of menhaden all similar	silvery with brassy sides, fins pale yellow, dark shoulder spot, numerous small spots behind bluish green back. Resembles shad; dorsal and ventral deeply curved	to 14″; juveniles 3″–6″	bays, offshore; some enter freshwater rivers	Nova Scotia to Florida; other species, Gulf of Mexico, Texas

(cont'd.)

SPECIES	DESCRIPTION	SIZE	HABITAT	RANGE
Atlantic Thread Herring (*Opisthonema oglinum*) also known as greenies	Dorsal slightly curved, ventral deeply curved. Silvery with greenish back, 6–7 dark streaks on side, dark spot above opercle, larger dark spot behind	to 1'; juveniles 1-1/2"–4"	bays and coastal waters, river mouths	Cape Cod to Bermuda and Gulf of Mexico to Brazil
Scaled Sardine (*Harengula jaguara*) also known as whitebait, shiners	Belly deep, dorsal relatively flat. Silvery with dark streaks on top that change color depending on angle of light, gray to gold to bright green	to 7"; juveniles 1"–3"	bays, estuaries, passes, coastal waters, river mouths	Florida, Bahamas, Gulf of Mexico to Brazil
Spanish Sardine (*Sardinella aurita*) also known as whitebait and shiners	shaped like a scaled sardine, but belly less deeply curved; same general color as scaled sardine	to 10"; juveniles 1-1/2"–3"	shallow waters, bays, lagoons, estuaries, river mouths	Cape Cod, Bermuda, Gulf of Mexico to Brazil
Tarpon Family Ladyfish (*Elops saurus*)	Silvery with bluish reflection on upper body. Long, thin, racy looking	to 3'; juveniles 3"–6"	bays, lagoons, especially mangrove areas	Cape Cod, Bermuda, Gulf of Mexico to Brazil
Porgies 155 species in this region; 1120 species world **Pinfish** (*Lagodon rhomboides*)	shaped like a bluegill, silvery with pale yellow-gold stripes, bluish brown above with eight faint bars	to 18"; juveniles 2"–4"	inshore, especially sea grass beds	Chesapeake Bay to Florida and Gulf of Mexico

(cont'd.)

SPECIES	DESCRIPTION	SIZE	HABITAT	RANGE
Dwarf Sea Bass Family 17 species this region **Sand Perch** *(Diplectrum formosum)*	perch-shaped, dark brown backs with alternating orange and blue horizontal lines	to 1'; juveniles 1-1/2"–3"	bays, coastal grassy areas and shallow banks	North Carolina, Bahamas, Gulf of Mexico to Uruguay
Snake Eels 21 species this region **Snake Eel** (generalized Family *Ophichthidae*)	Long, thin eel shape, cream, tan and olive for juveniles	to 30"; juveniles 2"–3"	shallow tropical seas	all tropical seas
Snappers 15 species this region **Schoolmaster** *(Lutjanus apodus)* other species red, tan, yellow	shaped like a largemouth bass, greenish brown, white belly, yellow fins, eight pale bars on side	to 2'; juveniles 2"–3"	sea grass beds, mangroves, shallow reefs	Massachusetts, Bermuda, northern Gulf of Mexico to Brazil
Spotted Tilapia *(Tilapia marlae)* African exotic, accidentally introduced in Florida, now widespread, two species	bluegill shape, brown bars, silvery sides to yellow and blue-green	to 12"; juveniles 2"–6"	coastal rivers to brackish bays	Africa coast, rivers of Florida
Toadfish four species this region **Gulf Toadfish** *(Opsanus beta)*	looks like sculpin, marbled and mottled brown, tan, white	to 1'; juveniles 2"–3"	sea grass beds, coastal bays, shallows along open coasts	Florida, Little Bahamas Bank, Gulf of Mexico

(cont'd.)

Naturals and Imitations

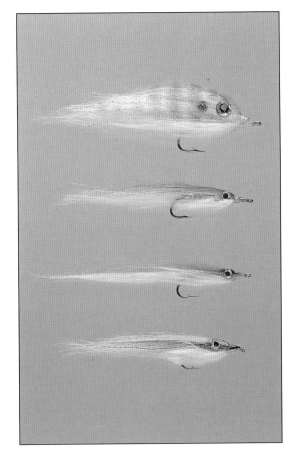

Pinfish
Atlantic silversides
American sandlance
Inland silversides

Silversides collected from Martha's Vineyard.

Sandlance collected from Martha's Vineyard.

TOP SIDE VIEW

Juvenile blue crab

Green reef crab

Black-fingered mud crab
(Bahamas)

Green porcelain crab

Smooth porcelain crab

Black-fingered mud crab
(Florida)

Juvenile blue crab

Green reef crab

Black-fingered mud crab
(Bahamas)

Green porcelain crab

Smooth porcelain crab

Black-fingered mud crab
(Florida)

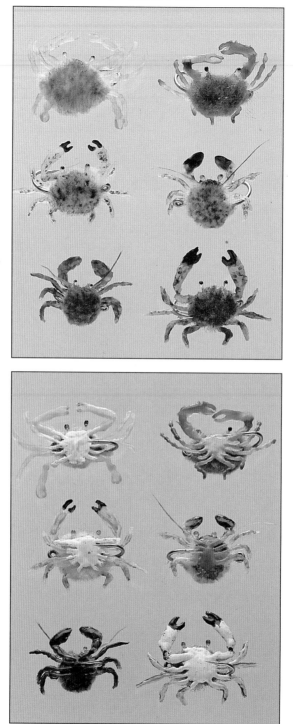

UNDERSIDE VIEW

Juvenile blue swimming crab collected from Coon Key Pass, Florida.

Green reef crab collected from Turneffe Reef, Belize.

Black-fingered mud crabs collected from Great Harbor Key, Berry Islands, Bahamas.

Casablanca blue crab collected from Ascencion Bay.

Smooth porcelain crab collected from Fakaunion Pass, Florida.

Black-fingered mud crab collected from Fakahatchtee Pass, Florida.

Pink snapping shrimp collected from Turneffe Lagoon, Belize.

White swimming shrimp collected from Venice Inlet. (Brown phase on left, gray phase on right).

Pink snapping shrimp
White swimming shrimp (tan phase)
Banded snapping shrimp
Juvenile spiny lobster

Banded snapping shrimp collected from Great Harbor Key, Berry Islands, Bahamas.

Brown snapping shrimp collected from shoreline of Cockney Key, Belize.

Various color shades of Mantis shrimp

White swimming shrimp (gray phase)
Hair shrimpy
Feather shrimpy

Dark mantis shrimp collected from Turneffe Reef, Belize.

Green mantis shrimp collected from Islamorada, Florida.

Simple white mullet
Don's baby mullet
Sea Devil
Swim-away fly

Gulf toadfish collected from Charlotte Harbor.

Butterfish collected from Martha's Vineyard.

Thread herring collected from Big Marco Pass, Florida.

Striped mullet collected from the Blackwater River, Florida.

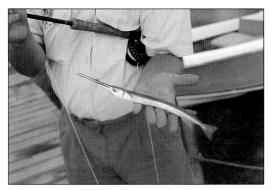

Needlefish collected from the Golden Bonefish Club dock, Cockney Key, Belize.

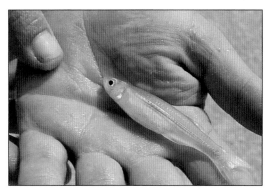

Striped anchovy collected from Goodland, Rabbit Key Pass, Florida.

Scaled sardine collected from Big Marco River, Florida.

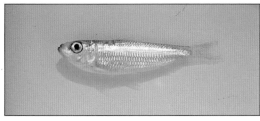

Spanish sardine collected from Big Marco River, Florida.

Anchovy collected from Big Marco River, Florida.

Striped mullet
Needlefish
Scaled and Spanish sardine
Bay anchovy

Winter prey for snook and tarpon
Male sailfin molly
Female sailfin molly
Striped majorra
Sheepshead minnow

Sailfinned mollies collected from the Blackwater River, Florida.

Spotfinned majorra collected from the Blackwater River, Florida.

FISH

SPECIES	DESCRIPTION	SIZE	HABITAT	RANGE
Mojara nine species this region **Spotfin Mojara** (*Eucinostomus argenteus*)	resembles white crappie, white with silvery reflection	to 4"	shallow coastal waters, sand, sea grass, mangrove channels	Bermuda, Florida, Gulf of Mexico, to Brazil, Pacific Mexico to Peru
Mullet six species **White Mullet** (*Mugil curema*)	dark above, brown, greenish or bluish silvery on sides; juveniles almost indistin-guishable	to 3'; juveniles 2"–7"	enters fresh water	worldwide in warm waters
Striped Mullet (*Nuqil cephalus*)	dark above, brown, greenish or bluish silvery on sides; juveniles almost indistin-guishable, but larger fish have black stripes	to 3'; juveniles 2"–7"	enters fresh water	worldwide in warm waters

SHRIMP

SPECIES	DESCRIPTION	SIZE	HABITAT	RANGE
Short-Clawed Sponge (*Synalpheus brevicarpus*)	Light green large claw, red-tipped	3/4"	lives in sponges	South Florida, Bahamas, Caribbean and West Indies
Long-Clawed Sponge (*Synalpheus longicarpus*)	Translucent cream with brown-tipped claws	7/8"	coral rubble and shells	South Florida, Bahamas, Caribbean and West Indies
Common Shore Shrimp (*Palaemonetes vulgaris*)	variable, translucent green with yellow and brown spots; translucent brown, and translucent cream	1-1/2"–2"	from freshwater tides, rivers, to saltwater bays, inlets	Chesapeake Bay to Brazil, Gulf of Mexico

(cont'd.)

SPECIES	DESCRIPTION	SIZE	HABITAT	RANGE
Arrow Shrimp (*Tozeuma carolinense*)	variable green, brown, purple in coral	2"	sea grass beds and coral	Florida, Caribbean, West Indies
Grass Shrimp (*Palaemonetes pugio*)	transparent, sometimes slight greenish tinge	7"	grass flats	Florida
Bumble Bee Shrimp (*Gnathophyllum americanum*)	yellow body with dark brown bands	4/5"	sea grass flats and coral	Florida, Bahamas, West Indies, Caribbean
Mantis Shrimp (*Squillidae*) 605 species **Common Mantis** (*Sequilla empusa*)	variable green, blue-green with darker green, blue margins, white with yellow to orange, eyes green	to 8"; juveniles 1-1/2"–3"	burrows in sand and mud from low tide, deep water	Cape Cod to Gulf of Mexico
Rock Mantis (*Gonodactylus oerstedii*)	dark mottled green or black, or cream with green mottling	to 4"	burrows in sand and mud from low tide, deep water	North Carolina to Brazil and Bahamas
False Sequilla or **Golden Mantis** (*Pseudosequille ciliate*)	yellowish brown, greenish brown, bright green, pale green or whitish	to 4"	burrows in sand and mud from low tide, deep water	South Florida, Bahamas to Brazil

Common Southern Commercial Shrimp Penaeus sp.

SPECIES	DESCRIPTION	SIZE	HABITAT	RANGE
Pink Shrimp (*P. duorarum*)	juveniles gray, white, green, pink, or colorless	8"; juveniles 1"–4"	all species migrate from offshore to grow up in grassy bays, mud bays and sounds	all species from northern United States south to Caribbean and South Atlantic
Brown Shrimp (*P. oztecus*)	juveniles light gray, light brown or spotted brownish	8"; juveniles 1"–4"		

(cont'd.)

SPECIES	DESCRIPTION	SIZE	HABITAT	RANGE
White Shrimp (*P. setiferus*)	juveniles translucent whitish with brown speckles, greenish, tannish	8″; juveniles 1″–4″		
Pink Spotted or **Brazilian Shrimp** (*P. brasilensis*)	juveniles brownish	8″; juveniles 1″–4″		
Mud Shrimp Infraorder *anomura* many species **Short-Browed Mud Shrimp** (*Callianassa atlantica*)	white with greenish and yellowish edges	to 2-1/2″	sandy mud intertidal to 100′	Nova Scotia to Florida
Flat-Browed Mud Shrimp (*Upogebia affinus*)	bluish or yellow-gray, sometimes a pink hue	to 4″	mud flats intertidal to 90′	Cape Cod to Florida
Snapping Shrimp (*Alpheidae*) many species **Common** or **Big-Clawed** (*Alpheus heterochaelis*)	dark translucent green with purplish side reflections	1-1/2″	soft mud, mangrove bays and oyster bays	Florida to Caribbean, Brazil
Banded Snapping Shrimp (*Alpeus armillatus*)	white with green or brown bands	2″	subtidal rocky and reef areas	South Florida, West Indies, Bahamas
Red Snapping Shrimp (*Alpheus armatus*)	reddish brown with golden reflections	2″	shallow coves and reefs	South Florida, Bahamas, West Indies

(cont'd.)

SPECIES	DESCRIPTION	SIZE	HABITAT	RANGE
Swimming Crabs (*Portunidea*) **Common Blue** (*Cellinectes sapidus*) two other species	white underside; immatures, carapace blue-gray to tan to medium brown; red and orange-tipped fingers	to 3-1/2"; immatures 3/4"–2", twice as wide as long	common on sandy, muddy bottoms, around oyster beds in bays and mouths of coastal streams, brackish water	Florida, Bahamas, West Indies
Swimming Crab (*Patuvus depressifrons*) two other species	mottled light to dark gray legs; bright purple or deep blue	1-1/4"; wider than long	shallow water with sandy bottom	Florida, Bahamas, West Indies, Caribbean
White and **Black-Fingered Mud Crabs** (*Xanthidae*) 165 species **Common Mud Crab** (*Panopeus herbetii*)	dark fingers; brownish green carapace, lighter under	1-3/4"	soft mud in oyster beds and around mangrove islands	Florida and Caribbean
Florida Mud Crab (*Cataleptodius floridanus*)	white or yellowish, red or brown spots, dark fingers	7/8"	muddy bays	South Florida and Caribbean
Spider Crabs (*Majidae*) many species **Green Reef Crab** (*Mithrax sculptus*)	medium to dark green with tannish brown legs and underside	1" oval shape	very common on reefs, shallow sand and grass flats; bonefish and permit feed heavily on these	Florida, Bahamas and Caribbean
Southern Spider Crabs (*Libinia dubia*)	dull brown	3", longer than wide	all bottom types, shallow water	Florida and Caribbean

(cont'd.)

CRABS

SPECIES	DESCRIPTION	SIZE	HABITAT	RANGE
Fiddler Crabs eleven species this region **Fiddler Crabs** (*Vca sp.*)	all species males have one very large claw; claws equal, color extremely variable even among same species, from dark mottled brown-green to light purple; lighter cream to tan-brown under	3/5″–1″	burrows above low water (intertidal) edge of marshes and mangrove swamp along rivers	very common from Massachusetts to Florida, entire Gulf of Mexico to South America, Bahamas

MARINE WORMS

SPECIES	DESCRIPTION	SIZE	HABITAT	RANGE
Segment worms (*Polychaeta*) 8,000 species **Polychaetes**	segmented bodies with bristly legs, every color under the rainbow; local collection necessary for color matching	2″–3′; most less than 6″	all types of shallow water bottoms	world

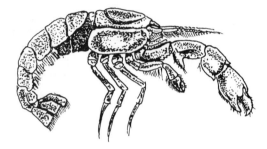

Mud Shrimp

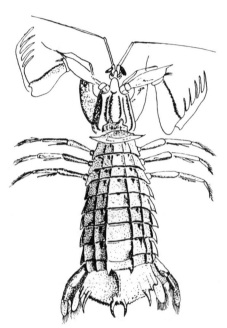

Mantis Shrimp

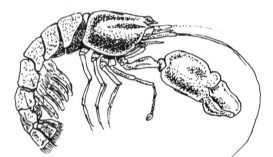

Snapping Shrimp

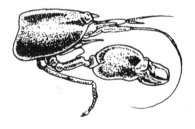

Swimming Shrimp

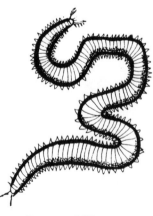

Segmented Worms

Green Reef Crab

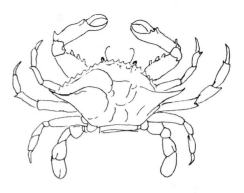

Blue Crab

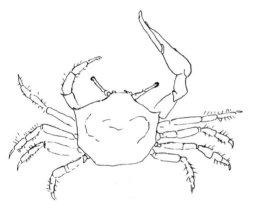

Fiddler Crab

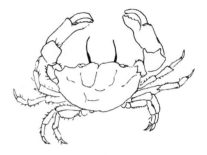

Mangrove Crab

Southern Spider Crab

Common Mud Crab

Bay Anchovy

Gafftopsail Catfish

Scaled Sardine

Hardhead Catfish

Spanish Sardine

Atlantic Menhaden

Ladyfish

Atlantic Thread Herring

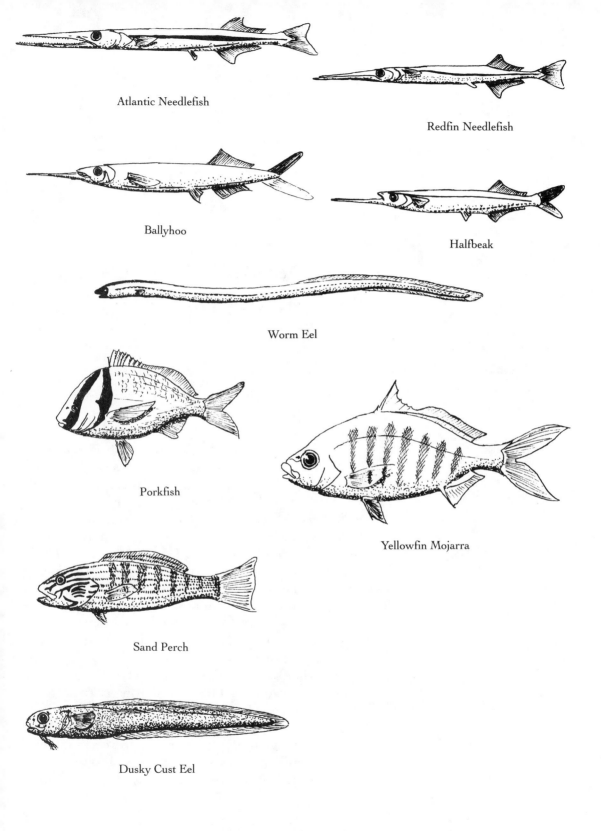

Atlantic Needlefish

Redfin Needlefish

Ballyhoo

Halfbeak

Worm Eel

Porkfish

Yellowfin Mojarra

Sand Perch

Dusky Cust Eel

6

Presentation — Tactics and Strategy

Proper presentation begins with good casting. To be successful in the backcountry, you must be a good caster. It is critical that you have the ability to consistently throw accurate, tight loops. This type of fishing is much more demanding than the typical "up north" trout and bass fishing. The tackle is heavier and the flies are larger and more air-resistant. There's more wind and longer casts are required. Quick delivery is often a must. Trout in a stream are stationary, and sometimes the same fish will live in the same area for years. It's quite a different story with most saltwater fish. They are much more aggressive and are constantly on the move. Sometimes they pass by so quickly there simply isn't time for false casting. In those situations, if you can't hit the moving target quickly enough, it's "bye-bye" until the next fish comes along. Some days you just don't get that many chances. You can't afford to waste those golden opportunities.

Casting, in our opinion, is at an all-time low. By that, we mean the percentage of good casters, compared to the total number of fly fishermen across the country, is lower than at any time over the past thirty years. There are several reasons for this. First of all, you'd guess that with all of the information available these days within books, videos, schools, clinics and seminars, that everyone should be an expert. However, that's not the case. For example, people seem to enjoy reading books and viewing videos on casting, but very few ever practice. You wouldn't dream of trying to become a par golfer without taking lessons and hitting hundreds of balls off the practice tee to develop a good stroke. For some strange reason, most fly fishermen don't approach casting the way they would to become proficient in any other sport. You've got to pay your dues on the casting field.

The increased popularity of "indicator" fishing has also contributed greatly to the demise of the accomplished fly caster. Last year, on a warm September day, we sat on the bank of the Big Horn River for two hours observing the passing armada, most of which were guides with their sports. Better than 95 percent were throwing indicators, some of which were about the size of a baseball. In one stretch we counted 54 consecutive anglers fishing with the brightly colored "bobbers." We realize that this is a deadly method that allows a beginning fly fisherman to get started in nymphing for trout, not to mention the pressure it takes off the guide (they love it). However, it leaves one embarrassingly short on the skills required to fish dry flies, streamers, and steelhead, salmon and saltwater flies. We get dozens of these anglers in our Florida schools and charters each year and find that most cannot begin to handle the casting until we've given them a lesson on the grass.

Lack of good instruction is another important factor limiting the development of better-than-average casters. Hopefully, the new certification program will solve this problem, but for now, it's mostly the blind leading the blind. Everyone wants to be a fly-casting instructor and many are hanging out their shingles; however, very few understand the mechanics and fewer yet are qualified to teach. Like other sports, there are some that perform well, but a very small percentage of those have the ability to transfer their skills to someone else. For example, both of us are avid skiers and, between us, we've had lessons from at least a dozen different instructors, all of whom skied beautifully, but only *two* stood out in our memories as being really competent as instructors. Teaching is not an easy job, especially teaching fly casting. It's the only sport we know of where a physical movement, the casting stroke, is totally reversed: one way for the backcast, then 180 degrees the other way for the forwardcast. If you think about it, the motions used for other sports, such as throwing, batting and swinging, are basically focused *forward*. This added element makes fly casting a little bit more complicated to learn—and teach. This is why the forwardcast and backcast should be learned separately and the backcast should be learned *first*.

HOW TO IMPROVE YOUR CAST

This is not a complete book on casting. However, it is important that we emphasize some of the basics, cover advanced techniques and show you how to practice so that you can fish the backcountry more effectively. For more information, read our book *Fly Fishing Strategy* and view the Scientific Anglers tapes on basic and advanced fly casting.

The first thing we must talk about is the wrist. Some instructors will actually tell you *not* to use the wrist at all. We feel that this is a big mistake because, in reality, the wrist is the most important element of the cast. You've heard the statement many times, "It's all in the wrist," and it's absolutely true. If you're into athletics at all, you'll understand the importance of the wrist in every sport, whether it's throwing or batting a baseball, swinging a club or racquet or shooting a basketball. All of these physical movements are quite similar. The arm works first and then the wrist. The arm basically sets up the proper position and initiates momentum. The wrist adds most of the power and accuracy. If you cast with the arm only, the rod simply won't load enough to put any zip into your cast and it will be very difficult to hit your target. Let's take baseball for a couple of examples. Can you imagine a pitcher throwing a ninety-mile-an-hour fastball or hard-breaking curve ball without using the wrist, or the center fielder making the throw to the plate without any wrist movement? Can't happen! Both players throw the ball by initiating momentum and getting the ball in the right position with the arm and finally making a superquick snap of the wrist for the power and accuracy needed.

Let's look at a fishing situation. You're standing on the deck of a backcountry skiff and must make a fifty-foot cast directly into a heavy breeze to cover a large tarpon. On top of the difficult conditions, you're using a 12-weight outfit with a 3/0 fly. Can you make this cast without snapping your wrist? No way!

All we're trying to point out is that the wrist *is* extremely important to the cast. It is the main source of power and it fine-tunes the accuracy. The problem with the wrist, and we imagine the reason some instructors tell you not to use it, is that you must learn to snap it quickly so that the rod tip moves in a straight line. Most beginners snap their wrist through too wide of an arc making the rod tip fall out of a straight line, causing a wide, wind-resistant loop. By quickening the wrist, the rod tip has less time to drop out of a straight line. The real top-notch casters have acquired, through lots of practice, what we call the "micro-second" or superquick wrist—just like the top athletes in any other sport. Why would fly casting be the only sport that doesn't utilize the wrist?

No matter what athletic endeavor you're involved with, whether it be golf, tennis, baseball, or basketball, the first thing you must learn is a good basic stroke. This is especially true with fly casting. The problem with this sport is that you really need to learn *two* basic strokes: one to the rear and one forward. As mentioned earlier, this aspect sets fly casting apart from other athletic movements which are mostly focused in the forward direction.

Work on your backcast first. It is imperative that you develop a good basic stroke to the rear before even thinking about working on the forwardcast. A good backcast is the foundation to having a good forwardcast. It is almost impossible to throw a poor forwardcast if the cast to the rear is properly made. The two most important elements of a good backcast are stopping the rod high and waiting until the line is straight behind you. This is basic information that most beginners are aware of, but it's amazing how not only neophytes but also more experienced casters allow their rods to go back too far and have bad timing. It is our observation that at least three out of four anglers have one or both of these problems. In our schools, we use what we call the "thumbs up" exercise to teach

"Thumbs-up" position

the proper backcast movement. Using the butt section of a rod, a pencil, a ruler or just pantomiming, perform the stroke to the rear, starting with the thumb parallel to the ground and ending with it straight up. With the thumb stopped dead at twelve o'clock, the rod is in perfect position. It's easier to watch your thumb than it is to keep track of the rod, especially when you're fishing. At first, use the arm only and make sure the thumb goes through ninety degrees, no more. When this motion becomes natural and the thumb always stops straight up, then you can start accelerating the movement, ending with a quick snap of the wrist. The amount of wrist snap should be about thirty degrees or less. This may sound like an oversimplified exercise, but you'll find it a bit more complicated than you think. It will probably take several hundred of these a day for a week or so to really engrain the stroke into your muscle system. Once you learn to do it properly, starting slowly and ending with a quick, but smooth, "pop" of the wrist, you're on your way to a great backcast. Reverse the movements and practice the same way for the forwardcast. Only after you've mastered both strokes do you finally put them together.

Coverage is the name of the game when it comes to backcountry fishing. Over the long haul, the number of fish you catch is directly proportional to the amount of water you cover. The angler who turns into the best "casting-retrieving machine" will definitely catch more fish, so a great deal of your effort on the casting field should be aimed at improving your shooting. There are three exercises that will quickly develop your ability to shoot more line. The first is the *long* shoot. Each day, put more line in the air, snap your wrist a little quicker and try to drive your rod tip in a straighter line. Within a couple of weeks you should be throwing at least seventy-five feet of line and possibly the whole ninety feet. Remember, shooting an entire fly line on the grass, without a fly and under ideal conditions, is quite different from actual fishing situations. If you can learn to consistently pick up thirty feet of line from the water and then, without false casting, shoot out to sixty or seventy feet with good accuracy and control, you're doing fine. The main benefit of long-distance casting is that the more line you put out, the more your errors are magnified. You can better make corrections once your mistakes are identified.

The second shooting exercise is the *short* shoot. Instead of starting with thirty to fifty feet of line or more, lay only ten feet out on the grass past your rod tip and perform the pickup and laydown cast. No false casting or shooting line on the backcast! This is very difficult as there is no mass or weight to bend the rod. Here's where you prove to yourself how important the wrist is. Since you don't have the luxury of all that line in the air to automatically load the rod, you must do it yourself by applying a superquick, "micro-second" snap of the wrist. One of the keys to good casting is developing the ability to bend the rod so that it can then unload and propel the line to the target. Your arm simply can't move fast enough to load a rod properly, but a lightning-quick flick of the wrist will almost bend it double. Ever try to crack a whip with only a movement of the arm? Nothing happens. Only a quick wrist can make the whip crack and only a quick wrist can make ten feet of line turn into twenty-five feet of line with a fly rod. This is not only a great exercise for training and conditioning your wrist, but it also teaches you the exact technique you need for handling the mangroves.

The final shooting exercise is the *back*-shoot, which was originally developed for our casting classes but has turned out to be the most valuable training technique for improving our own casting. The object here is to learn to shoot just as much line to the rear as you can forward. It may sound simple, but most casters who can easily shoot thirty feet of line on the forwardcast have trouble shooting five feet of line the first time they try to shoot backwards. There are two reasons for the difficulty: poor technique and poor muscle tone. Like the forwardcast, the final delivery cast to the rear must maintain a tight loop which, of course, is controlled by moving the rod tip in a straight line (stopping it *high*). Most casters drop the rod tip too low on the final thrust—remember your "thumbs-up" exercise. As for muscle tone, all other sports have required arm and wrist motions that are focused forward. In fly casting, we have to condition our muscles to work *both* ways, so we must work a little harder on the backcast. When you get to the point where you can shoot line just as easily to the rear as you can forward, you'll notice a tremendous upgrade in your total casting ability. A dynamic, tight loop backcast automatically shapes up the forwardcast.

If you could possibly spend an hour a day working on these three exercises, the *long* shoot, the *short* shoot and the *back* shoot, within a couple of weeks your shooting ability should be greatly improved. Here's a tip that will also help to speed your progress. Learn to observe your loops, both front and back, very closely while you practice. You'll notice that your false casts are much tighter than your delivery casts, so make a special effort to keep the final shooting cast as tight as possible. After all, the fish really don't care how well you false cast, they're only interested in how well you deliver the fly.

As you acquire the ability to shoot more line and fish farther from the boat, you must learn to adjust your casting stroke to compensate for *time* and *gravity*. The mechanics change a bit when you get into long-distance casting. With a really short cast, let's say a twenty-footer, it's very easy to direct your backcast straight behind you parallel to the water's surface and then come forward directing your forwardcast 180 degrees to the backcast. This situation, of course, complies with one of the basic rules of good casting—that the forwardcast and backcast should be in alignment with one another.

Now we'll look at how things change when the amount of line is greatly increased. Let's assume that sixty feet of fly line is picked up from the water and directed straight back, just like the twenty-foot cast. By the time all of this line has straightened, gravity will have worked on it so long that it will be out

Backcast with proper lift

of alignment with the intended direction of the forwardcast, not to mention the fact that it will undoubtedly slap the water behind the caster. To remedy this situation, you must learn to lift the rod on the backcast, directing the loop at an angle high enough so that by the time the line straightens, it will be properly aligned with the forwardcast. There is another very important benefit of the lift. The added weight of the longer line, sixty feet versus twenty feet, makes the rod bend more, causing the rod tip to fall during the power stroke. By lifting or raising the hand during the quick snap of the wrist, the rod tip stays up on a straight-line track, keeping the loop tight.

The amount of lift is determined by how much line you're handling, how high you want to throw it and how tight you want the loop to be, with two to three feet being the normal range. Raising the hand late in the casting stroke, precisely at the same time you snap your wrist, is the key to a really tight, dynamic loop. Be sure you stop in the thumbs-up position. Pantomime the motion before trying it with your actual rod and line. The *lift* is a dynamite technique and is a must for fishing the backcountry.

Step one of "the Lift" — beginning of stroke

Step two of "the Lift" — halfway through stroke

Step three of "the Lift"—final
position at end of stroke

How you stand and how you hold your rod may seem like
unimportant factors, but they are critical to efficient casting
techniques. By crouching and extending the arm forward and
down, you can easily keep the rod tip where it should be—on
the water. The only time it comes up is when you cast. Learn
to extend the casting arm as far as possible and cock the wrist
well forward. From this position, it's a "piece of cake" to make
a good pickup.

To complete your transformation into a "casting-retrieving
machine," practice until you can strip a whole fly line in about
twelve seconds. Trout and bass have a top speed of about fifteen miles per hour, while most saltwater species swim two to
three times faster. If you learn to put more "zip on your strip,"
you'll get more strikes, more hook-ups and greatly increase the
amount of water you can cover in a day's fishing. Hand dexterity is essential. The use of specialty casts, such as the reach
and curve, along with mending will be covered later in the
chapter.

EDGES

Knowing *where* to cast is just as important as knowing *how* to cast. You can be the greatest caster in the world, but if you don't throw your fly to the right spot, you won't catch fish. Learning to recognize "edges" will vastly improve your ability to cast into areas that have the greatest potential of holding fish. Edges are areas where two environments meet or come together. They provide either food, shelter, comfort or an ambush point, or a combination of two or more of these factors. The greater the difference between these environments, the greater the fish-finding potential. Some of the more common edges are areas where:

— Fast water meets slow water;
— Shallow water meets deep water;
— Clean water meets dirty water;
— Light bottom meets dark bottom;
— Shaded water meets sunlit water.

Excellent edges are formed by natural structure, such as:

— Logs and limbs;	— Sand bars;
— Fallen trees;	— Grass and vegetation;
— Brush piles;	— Drop-offs;
— Oyster bars;	— Weedlines;
— Shoals;	— Depressions in the bottom;
— Rocks;	— Springs.

And, man-made structures such as:

— Canals;	— Jetties;
— Walls;	— Channel markers;
— Docks;	— Piers.
— Bridges;	

One of the most important concepts in locating fish is to concentrate on *points*, *pockets* and *passes* — the basic "three P's" of finding fish in the backcountry. Points are especially good because the current during tidal movement speeds up around the protruding mangroves creating a funneling effect that brings more food to the area. During spring tides, these edges are a mecca for hungry snook and redfish. Pockets, or depressions, in the mangroves form shaded edges that become excellent

Fishing a shadowed pocket

Classic mangrove point

Typical mangrove shoreline with well-defined wind line

ambush stations, and passes not only move tremendous amounts of food but also act as a superhighway for all species of fish during maximum current flow.

Wind lines create edges that you *never* want to pass up, particularly when they form off points or at the mouth of a pass that empties into a shallow bay. More subtle edges such as those formed by pH factors and fish themselves should be considered. The three most common edges of all are the surface of the water, the bottom and the shoreline.

In order to develop the ability to find fish successfully, you should:

❶ Learn all you can about tides and how to interpret the tide atlas.

❷ Study charts of the area you want to fish.

❸ Know as much as possible about the habits of the fish.
❹ Visit local fly and bait shops for information.
❺ Teach yourself to identify edges. Learn to "think like a fish" and you'll become a much better angler.

TACTICS

There are many types of water that make up the full spectrum of backcountry fly fishing. In order to simplify matters, we'll discuss the tactics we use for five water types:

❶ The Mangroves
❷ Outside Beaches, Passes and Points
❸ Inside Bays and Passes
❹ Rivers
❺ Man-made Structures

THE MANGROVES

Fishing the mangroves is what you think about when you think of backcountry fishing. The water is very shallow, usually one to three feet deep, and there are literally hundreds of mangrove islands, both large and small. Mangroves are everywhere. They provide more cover than you can imagine. In fact, there are so many places for a fish to hide that you expect a strike on every cast. It's the "fishiest" looking water you'll ever see. That's what makes it so interesting. You never know whether a tiny nine-inch snapper or a twenty-pound tarpon is going to dart out and grab your fly. Snook, jack crevalle, redfish, sheepshead, ladyfish, trout, barracuda or permit can show up at any time. Even when the fishing is slow, there's other wildlife that keeps things interesting: birds such as herons, ibis, egrets, spoonbills, eagles, ospreys, woodstorks, cranes, cormorants and pelicans, along with dolphins, manatees and the occasional alligator. Numerous oyster bars provide a mecca for fish-attracting critters like shrimp, minnows, worms, crabs and other crustacea.

Fishing around an oyster bar

The best time to fish for snook in the mangroves is normally during the peak flow of a falling tide. Water rushing out of the roots brings with it all kinds of food and the fish really get turned on. The higher the tide the more goodies are flushed out. A fast incoming tide can be good too, but sometimes if it moves too fast, the fish quickly bypass spots that would normally be good. They act like they're in a hurry to explore the newly exposed areas back in the roots. The outgoing flow concentrates the greatest amount of food for the longest period of time. This condition usually produces the best fishing. At extreme high tide, finding fish can be a tough proposition. They're so far back in the mangroves that it's almost impossible to get their attention. At low tide they are either widely dispersed or have left altogether, headed for the nearest hole or pass.

Sight fishing for snook is exciting but, due to heavy cover and murky water, is rarely possible in the mangroves. Blind casting perpendicularly to the bank is the normal method. The key to success in this type of fishing is coverage. The angler who covers the most water will certainly catch the most fish over the long haul. Depending on the speed of the boat, a cast should be made every five to twenty feet along the shoreline, the more the better. Here's where casting efficiency and accuracy are of utmost importance. Time is money, so false casting should be eliminated. You should work on your shooting so that you can pick up twenty feet of line and immediately fire it back out to forty feet or more without a false cast.

Be sure to give special attention to *points* and *pockets*. These are the places that are most likely to hold fish and deserve the best coverage. Points can be great hotspots during maximum tidal flow and should be covered accordingly. Start focusing your attention ahead of the boat as you approach a point, giving it a few extra casts and being sure to cover the area the boat will be going through. Many times fish (sometimes very good ones) will be feeding ten to thirty feet off the point. If you don't cast ahead, you'll merely spook them instead of catching them.

As mentioned earlier, the normal method of fishing the mangroves is to cast perpendicularly to the bank. If the boat is moving along at a three- or four-mile-per-hour pace, probably the best you can do, assuming you're a fairly efficient caster, is hit the bank every fifteen to twenty feet. This is pretty good

Excellent snook cover

coverage, but you can do a lot better with a *parallel* retrieve. In fact, this mode of presentation is deadly. It is accomplished by using either a reach or curve cast, extreme mending or any combination of the above. The object is to "paint" the contour of the shoreline with the cast, keeping the fly line as close to (or even under) the mangrove branches as possible. During the retrieve, the fly is covering the *entire* shoreline instead of just a small percentage of it. Points are best covered by using a positive curve followed by mending. As you approach the point, throw a cast that curls around the mangroves, putting the fly on the far side, then immediately mend excess line tight to the shoreline on the near side. This technique "wraps" your fly line completely around the point and allows maximum coverage. It works best from the bow of a boat that is being poled or propelled forward.

The reach cast, which is much more accurate and easier to control than the curve, is great for increasing your parallel coverage. Combined with mending, it will keep your fly closer to

Parallel coverage with reach cast

Casting in a mangrove

the mangroves for a much greater period of time. You'll be surprised, once you start thinking in terms of *parallel* coverage instead of the conventional *perpendicular* coverage, how much more time your fly will be where it *should* be—along the "edge" of the mangroves. Fished from a small craft like the Water Otter, this technique is the deadliest method of all for catching fish that are lurking under the mangroves. The Otter is a twenty-pound boat that can be propelled by flippers, oars or a motor, either electric or gasoline. We just use the flippers while we're actually fishing. The big advantage over all of the other craft we've tried (canoes, rowboats, and rubber rafts) is that it's totally quiet and makes a minimum disturbance. It's a real "stealth machine." You can get right on top of the fish and they don't know you're there. This, of course, allows you to fish very close to the mangroves, sometimes only ten to fifteen feet away. By using the parallel system—reach casts with lots of mending—your fly is always right on the edge. We've caught snook up to fifteen pounds and forty-pound baby tarpon with this technique. Fish of this caliber caught from a twenty-pound boat are a real blast.

Parallel coverage from
Water Otter

The fish are not always hiding under the mangroves. There are times when they are swimming freely, well out from the branches. It all depends on the tide. A good rule to remember is that the higher the tide, the tighter the fish will be to the mangroves, and the lower the tide, the more dispersed they'll be. A superhigh spring tide will attract the fish way back into the root system where lots of fresh goodies will be available for them to gorge on. During those periods it's almost impossible to get their attention. At low spring tide, they'll either be spread all over the open water or will be hiding in the nearest hole, deep cut, or channel. Basically then, at higher water levels you'll fish tighter to the mangroves with short, pinpoint casts aimed right at the edge of the leaves. At lower levels, you'll fish farther out using much longer casts, trying to cover as much water as possible.

You have the choice of moving along with the tide or against it while you're fishing. More often than not, you'll want to move with it partly because it's easier to pole or motor the boat in that direction, and if you're into fish, you might as well glide along with them. Finding that magical stage of the tide when you have good lively flow and a depth of about one-and-a-half to two feet can keep you in business for quite some time. The problem with this tactic is that you may be just ahead or just behind the fish you want to catch. If you're both moving along with the tide at approximately the same speed, you may never find them. In this situation, by working against the tide, you'll cover much more water and have a much better chance of intercepting them. Another advantage of working into the flow is that you'll automatically impart a much livelier action to your fly. This can be particularly helpful to anglers who have not yet learned how to put enough "zip in their strip."

Streamers are undoubtedly the best all-purpose fly for fishing the mangroves, partly because they can easily be tied to imitate the minnows and small fish that abound in the back-country, and partly because they can be stripped quickly through the water, a factor which is extremely important to good coverage. There are dozens of streamer patterns that work well and everyone seems to have a favorite. Ours is what we call the Sea Devil. It was not designed to imitate a specific critter, but instead to be a very impressionistic simulation of anything and everything. Besides being the "fishiest" looking fly you'll ever see, especially in the water where it really counts, it is constructed so that the tail doesn't foul. This may not seem like an important characteristic, but in reality, it's one of the most critical elements of a saltwater pattern. There's nothing as frustrating as having a fly that continually tangles, which always seems to happen when the largest fish of the day is swimming by.

We tie this fly mainly on 1/0 hooks in three colors: all white, pink-and-white, and yellow-and-white. It's a general imitation of various minnows and small fish, but probably best simulates finger mullet. The pink-and-white version looks like a bleeding fish, while the yellow matches the coloration of the fins of both snook and jacks. If we had to pick one of the three colors to fish exclusively, it would be the pink-and-white model. In fact, a tube of bright reddish pink lipstick is a staple item carried in our tackle box, just in case we run out of the pink-and-white flies. Lipstick works beautifully in "spiffing up" the all-white patterns.

Various speeds of retrieval can be used, but normally faster is better. Saltwater fish swim very fast, much more rapidly than freshwater species, and so do the minnows they feed on. To simulate this action, you must move your fly in a lively manner. The normal stripping motion is fifteen to twenty inches long and is done at a pace of one to one-and-a-half strips per second. The key to good stripping is the same as for good cast-

Final position after quick
wrist snap

ing—a superquick snap of the wrist. The arm simply can't
move fast enough to load a fly rod properly. Likewise, you
can't impart a dynamic lifelike motion to your fly by using the
arm only. Learn to use your wrist for stripping.

Try to fish your streamer at the depth of the fish. This factor becomes more important as the water gets deeper. At a
depth of a foot or less the problem is not nearly as critical as it
is at three feet. Fish will move up or down to take a fly but are

Final position after quick wrist snap of both wrists

much more cooperative when it is presented at their level, and you'll notice that your hook-up percentage goes up too. Under certain conditions such as extremely cold water and slack tides, you have to put the fly right in their mouth. One of the many pitfalls of fishing with a high rod tip is that the fly rides a little too close to the surface, resulting in "lookers" but not many "takers."

One of the deadliest retrieval techniques is to let your streamer sink all the way to the bottom and then strip it quickly and erratically so that it climbs towards the surface. This covers all levels and can induce violent strikes, some right at the surface as you start to make your pickup for the next cast. The fly appears to be making a frantic escape and triggers a quick decision.

A jiglike effect can be accomplished by adding a weight to the shock tippet right at the eye of the hook. This is similar to the popular method used by trout fishermen of adding a split-shot to the head of a Woolly Bugger. In this case, however, we use a lead sleeve which is simply slid over the tippet before tying on the fly. The sleeve is a small tube and can't fly off like split-shot can. With this system you can impart an incredibly tantalizing movement to your fly if you learn how to coordinate both hands. Again, the key is using a superquick movement of the wrist—in this case, *both* wrists. With the rod hand, pop your wrist upward and at precisely the same time, pop the wrist of your line hand downward, stripping eight to ten inches of line. If timed perfectly, the combination of a vibrating rod tip and a short fast strip will make your fly come "alive." Remember, use the wrists only—your arms are stationary.

You can make your fly swim right or left, or anywhere you want, if you have the ability to mend line properly. To swim your fly to the right, for example, make a mend in that direction and the fly will move to the right when you strip. Good mending technique coupled with the fact that the fly goes where the line goes allows you to make some "magical moves" with your retrieve. If you want to create a back-and-forth movement, there are several ways to do it. The simplest would be a single mend to the right followed by a strip, then a mend to the left followed by another strip. Another method would be two, three, four or more mends to the right, each followed by a strip, and then the same procedure to the left—or two, three, four or more mends to the right followed by only one strip and then the same to the left. The combinations are endless. You can even make the fly swim *away* from the boat if you "shoot-mend" properly. This technique is valuable when there's a good chance of spooking the fish. If you're having trouble with mending, concentrate on the quick wrist. It's almost impossible to make good mends with the arm.

While on the subject of retrieving, it should be mentioned that continual stripping, hour after hour, is very abrasive on your fingers. To save yourself a lot of misery, it's smart to have a glove for the rod hand or at least some protection for the stripping fingers. Garden gloves made of synthetics, not cotton, do an excellent job and are inexpensive. If you want to cover the stripping finger or fingers only (some anglers use one, some two), you can use an item called a rug weaver's thimble. It's a leather finger and can be found in most sewing shops. You can also use Band-Aids but they don't last long.

No matter how well you cast, your fly will occasionally get hooked up in the mangrove trees and brush piles. The natural reaction when this happens is to immediately snap the rod into a vertical position with the hope of jerking the fly out of the branches. Sometimes it comes out and sometimes it doesn't. When it doesn't, you're at high risk of breaking your rod. Even if it does, the line, leader, and fly will often sail back into your face leaving a tangle from hell that puts you out of commission for a long period of time. The proper way to remove your fly

The "Fluter"

from the mangroves is to point your rod directly at the fly with both arms fully extended and all the slack stripped out. Then, *gently* pull the rod by *slowly* bending your arms. If the fly falls to the water—and 80 percent of the time it will—simply fish it as usual. If not, pull harder, all the while keeping the rod pointed directly at the fly. If that doesn't work, you'll have to go in. It's better to lose a fly than to break an expensive rod.

Fishing the mangroves with surface flies is the most exciting type of backcountry angling. The topwater explosion of a large snook, jack or baby tarpon is about all your heart can stand, especially when it happens close to the boat in a quiet shallow area. Recently, we hooked and landed a forty-pound tarpon under these conditions. The fish took a Chartreuse Fluter, our favorite surface fly, while we were fishing the edge of the mangroves in a small back bay just south of Naples. It smashed the soft foam popper less than fifteen feet away and in what seemed like a tenth of a second, jumped over the bow of the boat. Fifteen jumps and thirty minutes later, this silver beauty came to the hand and was released. This is about as good as it gets.

Topwater fishing is usually best when the water temperature is between 75° to 80°, which is pretty much the preferred feeding range of snook and most other backcountry species. Below 70°, their metabolism is so low that they're not quite as willing to eat on the surface, although we have caught numerous jacks and a few redfish when the water temperature was in the 60° range.

The new soft foam poppers have made a tremendous impact on topwater fishing. Until recently, poppers and sliders were made of very hard materials, usually wood, while hairbugs and divers were fashioned out of deer hair. Each has its advantages and disadvantages. Wood is durable, floats well and makes plenty of noise to attract fish, but has an unnatural feel resulting in many missed strikes. Deer hair produces a much higher hook-up percentage because it looks and feels so natural. However, it lacks good durability, flotation, and noise-making qualities. Soft foam has all of the advantages and none of the disadvantages of the other two materials. It floats like a cork, has an excellent sound in the water, feels soft and yummy and is almost indestructible. It even hangs up less in the mangroves because it's so light. Light as a feather, it doesn't have the inertia that causes heavier materials to spin and tangle around the branches.

Soft foam poppers and sliders are great, but the Fluter design seems to be the deadliest design of all. It's shaped more like a slider than a popper and the nose has a slightly blunted shape. The most important features of the Fluter, however, are the three flutes, or grooves, in the head, which shoot small amounts of water over the top and out each side of the fly. Its outstanding effectiveness is probably due to the fact that it kicks up a "more natural" fuss in the water than standard poppers and sliders. It may also have something to do with its unique shape and an action the fish haven't seen before. Most of the credit for this creation goes to Captain Bob Marvin of Naples, Florida.

Poppers and Fluters work well in many situations but can be especially effective during higher tides when the fish are under the mangroves. In fact, there are times when the noise factor made by a surface fly is the only way to induce a strike. To carry this a step further, we often false cast in such a manner that our fly slaps the water, making as much of a disturbance as possible. This is done one, two, three or more times before the fly is allowed to settle on the water. The object is to make enough noise to get the fish to come out from under the branches to see what's going on.

In extreme low-water conditions, let's say a foot or less, noise-making surface flies can save the day. Where a streamer

Popper Dropper

would have to be stripped at high speed to keep it from hanging up on the bottom, you can fish a Fluter any way you want. A method that often works well is to make the cast, quickly make a lot of noise with three or four strips and then wait. You may be amazed how far a snook or red will move to take the fly.

Now, let's take a look at what we feel is the deadliest rig in the ocean. We call it the "Popper-Dropper" system and it consists of two flies: a popper as the lead fly and a streamer as the tail fly. You've probably figured out the rationale already. It's pretty simple. The popper does the attracting and the streamer does the catching. Not always, though. Some days the popper catches more than the streamer. The good news is that this system is absolutely dynamite as far as catching fish is concerned. It *should* be. It's combining the best of both worlds. The bad news—only if you're *not* a good caster—is that it has more wind resistance and is a little harder to handle.

The rig is easy to set up. After tying a loop knot to the eye of the popper, tie two feet of shock tippet to the bend of the hook with a clinch or similar knot, and then add the streamer with another loop knot. You can try all kinds of combinations: popper to popper, streamer to streamer, or whatever. Actually, the twin popper combo is dynamite when you get into a school of ladyfish. You'll get lots of doubles.

Another method of fishing a popper or hairbug is to fish them on a sinking line or a mini lead head, which is a short piece of leaded line that is tied into your leader. When you strip, the fly is pulled towards the bottom, and when the pressure is taken off it rises to the surface. This is a good method for covering a variety of levels but not much fun to fish.

Flies that swim backwards are effective when the tide is in its higher stages and the fish are "camped" under the mangrove branches. The key to presenting these flies is being able to throw very accurate slack-line casts and to immediately feed a few extra feet of line out your guides as soon as the fly hits the water. You *need* the slack to allow the fly to swim away from you. These patterns are also deadly fished under docks, boats and bridges, especially at night.

Before leaving the subject of flies, we want to stress the importance of sharp hooks. Always carry a hone and make sure you keep the point sharp enough so it won't drag across your thumbnail. It doesn't matter if you triangulate, which is the most popular style of honing, or if you make two or four cutting edges, just keep your hooks sharp. To keep the points from rolling over and breaking down, remember to file *towards* the bend of the hook, *away* from the eye. If you don't have time to do the filing, then get one of those battery-operated hones. They do a relatively good job and are quick.

One of the biggest mistakes made by the neophyte fly fisherman is picking the rod up before the fish can eat the fly. We admit that this is a very difficult habit to break, but it must be done. This is one aspect of saltwater fishing that's impossible to teach—you must experience it. That's why we feel it's critical that students in our schools get most of their training on the water under real fishing conditions. You can try to describe what it's like to have a big redfish or tarpon swim up behind your fly, but until this experience is actually encountered, it's hard to comprehend.

Before you can hook a fish, you must be in the proper position. After the cast is made you should be standing square to your target with knees slightly flexed for good balance and your upper torso bent forward from the waist. The casting arm

is fully extended with the wrist cocked downward as far as possible. This position should bring the rod tip right down to the water. Your line hand should have all the slack stripped out. This is the perfect position for hooking, striking and picking up line for the next cast.

Let's assume, after three or four strips, that a big redfish comes charging up behind your fly. (We'll use reds for our example because they are the most difficult to hook, the reason being that they move slowly and are highly visible.) As the redfish moves in, he'll flare his gills, turn a pretty coppery red color and finally inhale your fly. Most beginners will have done one of two things by this time, both of which are wrong. Either they will have totally stopped stripping in awe of this great show put on by the redfish, or they will have reacted violently, yanking the fly out of the water. If you stop stripping, the fish will rarely take the fly. He'll just swim off. If you yank the fly out of the water, you'll hardly ever hook the fish, as this is the worst hooking angle you could possibly have.

What should you do in this situation? Keep the rod tip down and keep stripping at the same pace until the redfish picks up the fly and starts swimming away with it. When he turns sideways and you feel the line tighten, you can set the hook with a horizontal sweep of the rod, pulling in the opposite direction the fish is traveling. Quite often, the fish will set the hook for you if you've kept your rod tip low and continued to strip. Now that the redfish is hooked, you can forget him for a moment and go to work on clearing the line. First, look at the loose line and make sure it isn't tangled around your feet or any obstructions in the immediate area. Then form an O-ring with the thumb and index finger of your line hand and feed the line smoothly into the stripper guide. When all loose line is cleared, you can come up with the rod to about 45 degrees. If you were fighting a tarpon, you'd come up higher so you'd have plenty of room to lower the rod on a jump. Since reds don't jump, you can use a lower fighting angle. If the fish makes a wild, uncontrollable run, take your hand off the reel handle and point the rod directly at him to keep friction out of the system. When he slows down and can be controlled, pump him towards you by raising the rod and then cranking in the slack as you lower the rod. One of the keys for subduing a fish quickly is to constantly keep him off balance. When he goes one way, you put pressure on the other way. Proper technique is much more important than brute strength. When the fish finally arrives at boatside, be gentle and try to remove the hook as quickly as possible. You can handle a redfish by gripping his outer gill covers with your fingers or better yet, just slide your hand under his belly to control him as you remove the hook. Don't stick your fingers up inside the gills or you'll run into some sharp bony plates. With snook, you can put your thumb inside their mouth and hold them vertically, much like you'd handle a largemouth bass. Don't hold them horizontally by the mouth, especially large snook, as you may inflict some serious damage to their lower jaw structure. Be careful of their gill covers; they can cut like a razor blade. Jack crevalle also have something to hurt you with: two tiny, but extremely sharp, spines that project out from next to the anal area. Small jacks can be handled by wrapping your hand around the top of their head and squeezing the gill covers. Large jacks can be tailed, but it's advisable to wear gloves.

If you want to know how much a fish weighs, all you have to do is make two quick measurements, length and girth, before you release it, then plug those figures into the following formula:

$$\frac{\text{GIRTH}^2 \times \text{LENGTH}}{800} = \text{WEIGHT IN POUNDS}$$

For example, a 25-inch snook with a girth of 14 inches:

$$\frac{14 \times 14 \times 25}{800} = \frac{4900}{800} = 6.1 \text{ pounds}$$

To release a fish properly, hold him level in the water and move him back and forth until he is able to swim off under his own power.

OUTSIDE BEACHES, PASSES AND POINTS

You never know what you'll find when you fish the outside edges of the backcountry—baby tarpon rolling in the passes, giant snook spawning along the beaches, big jacks and reds ambushing bait around the points, gigantic schools of Spanish mackerel, ladyfish, or bluefish feeding in the open water, or one-hundred-pound tarpon traveling the coastline. Be ready for anything. You will need a 10- to 12-weight rod for the large tarpon and a 7- or 8-weight for the smaller fish, along with thirty-pound to eighty-pound shock tippets and wire leaders for the "toothy critters." Poling, drifting, anchoring, and wading are all important aspects of this type of fishing. An electric motor is indispensable.

Unlike mangrove fishing, which is often done in murky or swamp-stained conditions, outside fishing is normally done in beautiful, clear water. This allows a greater chance for sight fishing, which adds an excitement factor to the sport. Unfortunately, it can also cause a real problem for the inexperienced. Casters who can handle eighty feet of line on the practice field suddenly turn to jelly when a jumbo-sized fish is spotted in clear water. We see this happen all the time. The problem is rushing the backcast, and it's something you must work on if you want to become a good saltwater fly fisherman. In most sight-fishing situations, you must present the fly with great speed, but no matter how quickly the cast must be made, *never* rush the backcast. If the backcast doesn't straighten, the forwardcast doesn't have a prayer. This is, without question, one of the biggest reasons that neophytes have so much trouble when they are introduced to the salt.

Tarpon start showing up along the outside beaches and passes when the water temperature begins to climb above the 75° mark. Most of the time they are easy to spot, especially when they're rolling with a good portion of their body coming out of the water. Sometimes, however, their rises can be more subtle with a dorsal fin barely showing and looking like a knife blade slicing through the surface. In choppy conditions this can be difficult to see. Shallow rolls generally indicate that tarpon are running high or staying near the surface, while high arcing rolls mean they are traveling low along the bottom. The closer they are to the surface, the greater the possibility of getting a fly in front of them. When they are swimming deep, it is extremely difficult to get their attention.

Assuming there is more than one fish within your casting range, the first thing you must do is pick out the fish you want to cast your fly to. Unless the lead fish is much bigger than the others, you're probably better off throwing at one farther back in the school. If you cast to the leader, he'll undoubtedly bring the whole pack with him when he follows your fly and if he doesn't take, all the fish are likely to flush. There's nothing more frustrating than blowing out the entire school on the first cast. If you have a choice, pick a fish that is fifty feet away rather than one that is only twenty-five feet away. Do everything you can to keep the tarpon from seeing the boat. Once they're aware of your presence, it's a tough ballgame. Bend at the knees and at the waist to keep your profile as low as possible.

There are two important principles to remember when presenting your fly to a tarpon, or for that matter any saltwater fish. First of all, cast your fly in such a manner that when you make your retrieve, it will swim in the same direction the fish is moving. They are more likely to chase a fly that is attempting to escape rather than one that is attacking them. If your casting angle makes this type of retrieve impossible, your second choice is a cast that allows you to strip the fly at some angle, either right or left, to the direction the fish is swimming. Quite often their prey will dart off to the side rather than moving straight ahead. A fish swimming directly away from you creates the worst casting angle of all. This results in a retrieve that brings the fly head-on into the fish. However, you can alleviate this problem by using a reach or curve cast. Instead of casting directly over the tarpon's back, use a cross-body reach cast to lay the line off to the left (assuming you're right-handed) or a positive curve to lay the line to the right. Not only will you get a better angle of retrieve but you'll also reduce the possibility of the line spooking the fish. When you encounter fish that are daisy-chaining or milling around, be sure to cast your fly slightly to the outside of the rotating circle; to the left if they're swimming counterclockwise and to the right if they're moving clockwise.

The other important principle to remember when presenting your fly, especially to tarpon, is to be sure you get it down to the depth of the fish. Rather than move up or down to aggressively take your offering, they'll totally ignore it or follow it halfheartedly until they are spooked by the boat. Your hookup percentage is much higher when you fish at the right level.

Make the cast far enough in front of the fish and far enough beyond the "line of intercept" so that there's plenty of time for the fly to sink to the right level and end up at the right spot at the right time. Most beginners make the mistake of casting too close to the fish to allow proper presentation. In fact, quite often they cast so close that they spook the fish when the fly line hits the water. It is usually better to err on the side of casting too soon and too far than too late and too close. You can usually make the required adjustment with some quick stripping.

As soon as the fly hits the water you should have the line over the stripping finger (or fingers), the rod tip on the water, casting arm extended, and the wrist of the rod hand cocked well forward. This is the best position for retrieving the fly and setting the hook. It is also the most efficient position for initiating the next cast.

Use quick flicks of the wrist to strip the fly through the water. This imparts a much more lifelike action than can be produced by using the arm. The normal stripping procedure for tarpon is to move about fifteen to twenty inches of line per strip at a pace of one to one-and-a-half strips per second. When you see a fish come up behind your fly, there's two things you *must do* and two things you *must not do*. You must keep your rod tip down and you must keep stripping! You must not stop stripping and you must not pick up your rod tip! We cannot stress these points enough. If you stop stripping, the fish will lose interest and rarely strike. If you pick up your rod tip, you'll almost always yank the fly away from the fish.

Wait until the tarpon turns sideways and you actually feel the resistance to your stripping movements before setting the hook. If he swims to the right, set the hook by sweeping your rod tip low and to the left. If he moves left after grabbing the fly, sweep to the right. Moving your rod in this manner, in the opposite direction the fish is swimming, gives the hook an excellent angle of purchase. Keeping the rod tip low maximizes your chance for a hook-up even more. Remember, if you try to set the hook while the tarpon is still swimming towards you, the hook will slide out of his mouth 75 percent of the time. Be patient and wait for him to turn.

Even if you're successful in making the initial hook-up, the fly may still come out if you don't hammer it home. The interior of a tarpon's mouth is extremely hard and bonelike, making penetration very difficult. This problem is magnified even further due to the fact that relatively large flies, sizes up to 3/0 and 4/0, are used. The larger the fly, the tougher it is to penetrate, so after the first set you'll want to repeat the low sweeping motion several more times. Of course, one of the most important things you can do to increase your ratio of hook-ups to strikes is to keep your hooks as sharp as possible. Always carry a file and use it every time you change flies, especially when you're after tarpon.

The next step, once you've survived the initial hook-up, is to clear the line. Instead of watching the fish, direct all of your attention to the line that is jumping off the deck. Make sure it isn't tangled around your feet or any other obstruction. Form an O-ring with the thumb and index finger of your line hand and smoothly guide it into the stripper guide. Be sure to hold your O-ring at least one-and-a-half to two feet below the rod hand and keep the reel seat tight against your forearm, all the while keeping the rod angled at about 45 degrees. This system will prevent line from tangling around the rod butt or reel and will have your rod in a good position if the tarpon jumps during the clearing process. As soon as all of the line has been cleared, direct your attention back to the tarpon and raise your rod to a high angle of approximately 70 to 80 degrees. Your drag, by the way, should be set fairly light—one-quarter to one-third of the tippet strength.

By this time, Mr. Tarpon will undoubtedly be initiating a series of jumps. This is a period of uncontrollable frenzy, a time when you pretty much let the fish have his own way. Maintain smooth but light pressure in the system and keep a high rod. This puts you in position to lower the rod when the fish jumps. The reason for "bowing" to the tarpon when he jumps is two-fold. First of all, there is a tremendous difference in the amount of tension or pressure that a fish can create moving in the water versus moving in the air. Tail flips and head shakes are like lightning bolts when performed in the air, but are relatively slow under water. The high energy levels created by aerial acrobatics are much more likely to either pull the hook out or break the tippet. Second, if the fish falls back into the water on a tight line, it's likely to pop. By lowering the rod each time the tarpon jumps, you reduce pressure in the entire system. Learn to anticipate the jumps by watching your line closely. You'll notice that it normally begins to elevate in the water just before the fish explodes.

Double or multiple jumps, one immediately following another, can cause a problem if you're not prepared. After lowering the rod during the first jump, be sure to quickly raise it again so you're ready for the next one. When the first few minutes of panic and series of frantic jumps are over, you're ready to settle down and start fighting the fish in earnest. The first thing you might want to do is to be sure the hook is well set by hammering it home several more times.

Fighting fish properly is more of a matter of being smart rather than strong, although being in good shape is helpful. Just pulling hard will probably make you more tired than the fish will be. The best technique is to constantly change your angle of pressure. If he swims to the right, lower your rod tip to the water and pull to the left. Counter his mad dashes by quickly applying pressure in the opposite direction. The more often you make him change direction and keep him off balance, the quicker he'll tire. Drag can be fine-tuned by using your fingers to feather the line, by palming the spool, or both.

Work hard to land the fish as quickly as possible. The longer it lasts, the greater the chance of something going wrong, either the hook pulling out or the leader breaking. Try to keep the fish from taking out too much line, as the power of the rod is greatly decreased as line stretch increases. Long lines also create high tension in the system, especially when there's a big arc in the fly line. When you must follow the fish with your boat, don't pole or motor straight to the fish, but instead, aim at the spot where your line enters the water. A good rule of thumb is that you should be able to land a tarpon in approximately a minute per pound. If you take much longer, you're not doing a good job.

When you've brought the fish close to the boat, within twenty to thirty feet, try to finish the fight quickly so he can't get a second wind. Small tarpon can be controlled by hand; gloves are helpful, but you might want a gaff to control large ones. Remove the fly gently and then spend all the time necessary to revive the fish properly. A good method is to move the boat slowly while holding the tarpon alongside. The fish will swim away under its own power when fully revived.

Tarpon get most of the attention, but snook must also be considered as one of the prime targets when it comes to fishing the outside beaches and passes. Fishing for old "linesides" can be dynamite in these areas during late spring and summer. This is the time when big snook can be found feeding along the edges of major passes. Most of our biggest snook of the year are caught during this period.

These fish can be approached by boat or by wading. Walking along the beach is the best method for the beginning or intermediate caster. Snook in such areas of clear water are extremely wary and are easily spooked, so unless you can cast sixty to seventy feet, you'll end up spooking all the fish if you try them from a boat. It's not that they'll flush, but instead, they'll rarely hit your fly if they detect your presence. These fish don't get big by being stupid. By walking the shoreline, you can carefully sneak along keeping a low profile and get a pretty good shot at them.

During the lowest part of the tide, these fish will usually move into the deeper water of the nearest pass where you can wade along the edge, drift through in a boat or anchor up on the "downstream" side of the current. Quite often, most any fly will work, but sometimes a shrimp or crab imitation is necessary to simulate the naturals drifting through the pass. For beach fishing, the Deadly Eel is one of the most effective subsurface flies. However, during high tide in areas of heavy cover, the soft-foam Fluter can be dynamite.

Fishing the outside for school fish is not as exciting as fishing for tarpon and large snook, but can save the day when everything else is dead. During the winter months when the shallow water of the inside is barely holding in the low 60° range, the "schoolies" are sometimes the only game in town. If schools of ladyfish, Spanish mackerel, bluefish, small jacks, or trout are in the area, they are easy to find because of all the visual signs exposing them: birds diving, minnows flushing, and the fish themselves smashing bait at the surface. This type of angling provides a good introduction for the first-time saltwater fly fisherman. The casting is easy and there's lots of action. It gives the neophyte much-needed experience that will help him when going after other species.

Occasionally, schools can be fished by wading but the normal technique is to drift, pole, or motor your boat into range and start casting. Relatively small flies, sizes #2 to #6, work best on these smaller fish and multi-fly rigs can be dynamite. Try using twin soft poppers when you get into a heavy school of ladyfish and you'll have all the action you can stand, catching two at a time on the surface. If you find mackerel or bluefish, you'll have to tie on a wire tippet or your supply of flies will diminish quickly. If you get caught without wire, substitute *two* pieces of #15 mono. Most of the time these fish will not be fussy, but if they get selective or make lots of short strikes, drop down to size #8 or #10. Another technique that often works is to use a high visibility fly up front and a tiny dark-colored pattern for the trailer.

Points of land that extend out into major passes create a mecca for a wide variety of fish. Snook, redfish, tarpon, jack crevalle, sharks, trout, and many other species love these areas not only for the great concentration of food, but because they also provide an excellent place to ambush their prey. Points are easy to locate and easy to fish. When you become familiar with reading charts, you can pretty much pick out the best ones before you even fish unfamiliar water. The key is to learn how to recognize "funnel systems," which are areas where a large volume of water must push its way through a small opening to get to the other side. During peak tidal flow, the fish know that incredible amounts of food will come pouring past these points. Just like trout in a stream, they'll normally take up stations on the lee, or downstream side, of the funnel. From this position they can easily pick any morsel they want off the conveyor belt.

When the tide reverses, they switch sides.

Points are generally a piece of cake to fish. Unlike the mangroves where you must cover miles of shoreline to be effective, you can concentrate your efforts in a relatively small area. In fact, during heavy tidal flow, you will know precisely where the fish should be holding. The "edge" formed where the fast water meets the slow water on the downstream side of the point is the spot you want to cover thoroughly. The ideal place to position yourself for the best presentation, whether it be in a boat or wading, is in the quiet water on the lee side of the point. If the current is moving from right to left and you're right-handed, use an extreme cross-body reach cast (left reach) and as you strip the fly in, keep mending to the left. This method will keep the fly broadside in the current for the longest possible period of time, allowing you maximum coverage and keeping the fly at a good hooking angle. The easiest and most efficient way of imparting action to the fly when using this technique is to use what we call "strip and flip." After each strip with the left hand, mend or "flip" the rod with your right hand. Both movements, if done with superquick flicks of the wrist, give a lifelike action to the fly. Always flip in the direction that will keep the fly line perpendicular to the current—in other words, to the left, if the flow is going from your right to your left. Your body should also be rotating to the left if you're flipping to the left.

When the tide is moving in the other direction, going from your left to your right, you need to throw a positive curve (one that curves to the left), a reach cast to the right or a combination of the two. Follow this with your "strip and flip" routine, in this case mending and rotating to your right. This method, by the way, is identical to the basic streamer technique used in a trout stream. You'll find that much of the technology that is used in fresh water can be applied to salt water. In fact, another streamer technique that we call the "dance" can be deadly. Instead of "flipping" in one direction only during the retrieve, flip back and forth, right, left, right, etc. and don't rotate your body. You can even stop stripping and just do the flip part. The combinations are endless. This type of motion "dances" the fly in an extremely tantalizing manner right in front of the fish.

When the weather is sunny and calm and other species are playing hard to get, we will often go looking for "tripletail." These funny looking creatures hang around buoys that mark

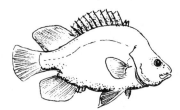

Tripletail

the crab traps. Most of the trap lines are a mile or so out from the main beaches, so you need a fairly calm day to go out in a small skiff. We put the sun to our back and run along the edge of the buoys to try to visually locate the fish. When one is spotted, we mark its position and return five or ten minutes later. By drifting in or using the electric motor, we get close enough to cast the fly within a foot or so from the buoy. They'll usually take if the cast is on target. The biggest problem is getting tangled up in the rope that connects the trap to the buoy. The fish know right where to go as soon as they grab the fly. A fifteen-pounder can give you quite a tussle on a fly rod.

INSIDE BAYS AND PASSES

Earlier in this chapter we discussed techniques for fishing the mangroves, and that's precisely what we meant: fishing *under* and in close proximity to the mangroves themselves. Now we'll talk about fishing the *open* areas of the inside bays, lakes and flats along with the waterways or passes that connect them. In watching other fly anglers fish the backcountry, it's amazing how few ever make a cast out away from the mangroves. It seems that most of them think it's a rule that you must throw toward the shoreline. In reality, there can be a lot of things happening in the open water.

Snook are the most sought-after gamefish in the backcountry, and popular belief has it that they're all hiding under the mangroves waiting to ambush the next passerby. Well, a good share of the time this is true, but they also spend a lot of time in open water. In fact, a few years ago, we had a great fishing experience where we released over forty snook in a two-hour period, all of which were caught anywhere from twenty to over a hundred feet out from the mangroves.

The reason the mangroves get most of the attention is undoubtedly due to the fact that they form such a "visual" edge to the angler. The cover and shade that they provide for the fish is so obvious. The more subtle edges are harder for the angler to see and therefore, harder to identify, especially at high tide. Most backcountry bays, however, are loaded with fish-attracting areas such as holes, ledges, depressions, vegetation, shoals, weedlines, and oyster bars. The best time to find them is at low tide, but you must be careful maneuvering your boat. It is best to use a pole for this type of exploration. It's not only safer, but you'll get a better idea of what the bottom is really like, its exact depth and texture. Variations in depth that form holes, depressions, and ledges may seem very insignificant to you, but can mean the world as far as finding fish is concerned. You can also learn a lot about the contour of the bottom by observing flow patterns as a fast-moving tide starts to come in. Much like the current in a trout stream, you can tell what the bottom is like by reading the surface.

The redfish is one of the prime targets of the fly fisherman in the open water of inside bays. They are the bonefish of the backcountry and in shallow water, are just as spooky. Instead of making long, fast runs like bones, they are known for short, powerful runs. However, on several occasions we've had them rip off a hundred yards of backing in quick order. The average fly-caught red runs six to eight pounds with ten to twelve pounders being fairly common. Recently we hooked up with a fish in the twenty-pound category that took off like a freight train. It was totally unstoppable, and after 175 yards of backing ran off the reel, the hook pulled out. Fish like this, even when you don't land them, are a great thrill.

Oyster bars act as a magnet to attract all kinds of goodies that redfish love to eat, including crabs, shrimp, scaled sardines, Spanish sardines, and various crustacea. Big reds, known as "bulls," are especially fond of finger mullet that can also be found near oyster bars, sometimes in great numbers. Most anglers feel that a rising tide produces the best fishing, but it has been our experience that falling tides are just as good. The main requirement is to be within casting distance of your favorite oyster bar during peak tidal flows. Reds are most active at these times, making them easier to spot and more aggressive when they feed. When redfish are on the prowl, they'll often come charging from twenty to thirty feet away to take a fly. They rarely miss when they're in this mode.

If there are no oyster bars around, you'll probably find redfish either foraging or traveling along the drop-off that runs along most flats. These ledges are usually very subtle, sometimes dropping only a few inches, but they form an edge that the fish feel comfortable in. Most often, this slight change in depth is found anywhere from twenty to sixty feet from the edge of the mangroves. The best way to locate these "redfish routes" is through close observation and experience.

Bays and flats that have an abundance of vegetation, especially turtle grass, may be the best areas of all for finding redfish. When spring tides wash bait back and forth through these "veggie beds," the fishing can be phenomenal. Shrimp, sardine and crab imitations all work well. The fish are easier to approach in this type of cover, and casting is not quite as critical as it is in the open sand-bottomed flats.

Once you've located a hotspot, you'd be smart to keep this information to yourself. Unlike most other saltwater fish, reds will often return to the same flat during the tacks same stage of the tide day after day and even stay in the same general area for several weeks. If you have a number of these spots located and you're the only one fishing them, you can keep a good thing going for a long period of time. Even then, don't pound an individual place too hard or you'll spoil it for yourself.

In shallow, murky water where visibility is limited, you may not see the fish itself, but it's hard to mistake the characteristic "V" wake made by a redfish as he feeds and meanders along the flats. They are real "wide-bodies" and tend to push lots of water. Much like bonefish, they like to stand on their head and forage for food on the bottom, digging out worms, crabs and other crustacea. In shallow water, the tail, which has a grayish blue cast, looks like a waving flag beckoning you to make a cast.

Accuracy is a must when casting to a tailing red. If your fly lands more than two feet away it's unlikely it will even be acknowledged, and if it lands two inches away it will probably spook the fish. Sometimes you can make a seemingly perfect cast and the fly will still go untouched because it got lost in a cloud of mud. The ideal situation is to have the fish working upstream or into the tide so you can cast into the clear water. This allows the fish to locate it and you're more likely to get a strike. If they are moving with the tide or foraging in a spot where there's no current, their visibility is limited by the mud. In this situation, you must keep making good casts until the fish finally sees the fly. One afternoon, we threw at a ten-pound red for almost half an hour before he finally inhaled a size #1 Shrimpy. This fish was feeding at dead-low tide and had created a mud wake larger than the boat. A tip on fishing for tailers, whether redfish or bones—unless the fish are superaggressive, don't use an epoxy-head fly. More often than not, you'll spook the fish on the first cast. They simply make too much of a disturbance when they hit the water.

Taking reds on the surface is a real kick. Hairbugs and old-fashioned wooden poppers work quite well, but the new soft-foam floaters are terrific. The one we call the "Fluter," in a chartreuse color, has taken more redfish than any other pattern over the past five years. The biggest problem fishing top-water flies for reds is picking up the rod and setting the hook too soon. You must be patient and learn to keep stripping with the rod tip glued to the water. Don't even think about picking up and setting until the fish has turned sideways and you feel pressure in the line. Actually, let the fish do most of the setting himself. The problem with redfish, more than with any other species in the salt, is that they are the "slowest and showiest" when it comes to approaching and striking a fly. Everything happens in slow motion and in vivid color. First of all, reds are highly visible in the water, so you normally see them approaching your fly when they're ten, twenty, or more feet away. As they make their unhurried approach, they flare their gills and "light up," their bodies turning a reddish copper color. By this time, most beginners have already snapped the rod up and yanked the fly out of the water. And the fish hasn't even touched the fly yet! If you've survived this long, continuing to strip with the rod tip down, you're in good shape, but you can still blow it if you're not patient. Due to the fact that your Fluter is high on the surface of the water, and the red's mouth is low, near the bottom of its head, the fish must go the extra mile to grab the fly. He must roll over and elevate his body halfway out of the water to be in position to get the fly into his mouth with any degree of purchase. To the angler, this dramatic display is very unnerving and seems to last for an eternity. Until you've gone through this experience a number of times, it's very difficult to keep from picking up the rod. Some beginners react the other way. They become spellbound at the whole process and stop stripping. Either way, you've blown a chance to catch Mr. Redfish.

Catching a large tarpon with a fly is considered by most as the ultimate thrill in saltwater fly fishing. Nothing can match the heart-pounding excitement of hooking into a 100-pound-plus fish that leaps like it was shot out of a cannon and takes two hours to land. We enjoy chasing these silver monsters of the flats as much as anyone else. However, for a steady diet, we'll take baby tarpon. By babies, we mean fish that weigh anywhere from five to fifty pounds, with twenty- to thirty-pounders being about average.

Even though we get a big kick fishing for the giant tarpon, one of the main pleasures of fly fishing is having action. Whether a fish is large or small, it's nice to have a bend in your rod every once in a while. Back in the good old days, in the late sixties and early seventies, it was almost impossible to spend a day on the flats without having at least three or four hook-ups. During those times, you felt crowded if you saw another skiff during an entire day of fishing. Now, of course, with lots of boats and very few manners, it's a whole different story.

Baby tarpon provide an excellent alternative to chasing the "big boys" on the famous tarpon flats of the Keys and Homasassa, and to be honest, are just as much fun to catch. Pound for pound, the babies are much more athletic and acrobatic. It can be compared to fishing for trout in Montana. The five-pounders are usually quite lethargic when compared to the sixteen-inchers. A forty-pound baby tarpon on a #8 weight rod will give you about as much fun and excitement as you can possibly find in the world of fly fishing. Most of these fish will jump ten to fifteen times and take about half an hour to land. When we fish for really small babies, five to ten pounds, we'll drop down to a #6 rod.

The main requirement for finding baby tarpon is a 75° water temperature. They can show up almost anywhere in the backcountry, but one of their favorite hangouts is where a pass joins an inside bay. The best time to be there is during the peak flow of a falling spring tide while the fast-moving water of the pass is funneling tons of shrimp and small baitfish onto the shallow flat. If this time period coincides with the first two hours of daylight, you have the perfect setup for baby tarpon. By studying your tide atlas and charts, you should be able to pick out these potential hotspots and be there at the right time.

These shallow flats are definitely our favorite places to fish for baby tarpon. With an average depth of only two feet, the fish are easy to spot and you can quickly get your fly to the right level. There's plenty of casting room and when you hook a fish, he must fly across the flat or go airborne. Another advantage is that the fish are pretty well dispersed over an area

Jack on Fluter

the size of a football field, so when you hook one, he doesn't blow out the rest of them. Typically there will be anywhere from ten to thirty fish on the flat, sometimes providing two to three hours of excitement.

The method of attack is pretty simple. Usually we just drift into casting range with an occasional adjustment with the pole or electric motor. The motor is much more practical, as it allows two anglers to fish at the same time, and in all honesty, provides better control. Things get pretty exciting when we get two hook-ups at the same time.

The Sea Devil, in pink and white, and the Shrimpy pattern, both in size 1/0, have been the best subsurface producers. The best topwater pattern by far has been a chartreuse soft-foam Fluter in size 1/0 and 3/0. When the water temperature is marginal, around 75°, we normally stick to the underwater flies. But when it rises to the 80° mark, we fish more on top.

These fish can be quite spooky when the tide gets low and the water is clear. Under these conditions, you may need to lengthen your leader to twelve feet or more. The ability to make long casts, at least sixty to seventy feet, is not only desirable but almost mandatory in these situations. You can sometimes get away with a thirty-foot cast when the fish are highly aggressive, but normally you've got to really bang it out there to produce.

Redfish and baby tarpon get most of the attention when it comes to fishing the open water of the inside bays. However, other fish can become prime targets on any given day. Sheepshead can be taken on a fly, but are difficult because they're so spooky. Just the shadow of a boat moving through an area sends them scurrying off, leaving a cloud of mud behind. The best bet for sheepshead is a small crab imitation. Let it sink to the bottom and then twitch it when they approach. A two- to three-pound fish will give you quite a tussle on a light rod.

Hardly a day goes by that you don't run into schools of small fish on the inside bays, whether they're jacks, ladyfish or trout. Foam poppers are excellent for these fish since the noise will keep enticing them to stay in the area. It's amazing how far a jack will travel to zero in on the "popping" sound of a topwater pattern. If you have trouble hooking these fish, make up a "popper-dropper" rig by adding a small white streamer to the rear of the popper hook. Remember, a school of jacks can move past you like a rocket, so the second you have them in casting range, get on them quickly. Most of the time these school fish will hit anything, partly because of the spirit of competition. Sometimes, however, they can be very selective because they're feeding on bay anchovies or some other tiny baitfish. For these situations, you may have to "match the hatch."

As far as the inside passes go, they mostly act as a funneling system to move food back and forth between the bays. They also act as a superhighway for the fish to travel inland during rising tides and to travel to the outside during a falling tide. Most of the time the fish are merely passing through, usually very quickly. There are a couple of exceptions. Some of the passes have deep holes or big depressions somewhere along their path. If you can locate these special places, either with your pole or depth finder, you have found a potential "honey hole" and you should check it out thoroughly. You'll probably have to anchor up and use sinking lines or weighted flies to see if it's a winner. If it is, don't tell a soul.

The other exception is when the water gets cold during the middle of winter and when it gets too warm during the middle of summer. Extremely shallow water, like the one- to three-foot depths found in most of the backcountry, is the first to be affected by temperature change. The deeper water found in the passes will maintain a more stable temperature and therefore offers a welcome refuge during extreme temperature changes.

RIVERS

Rivers are freshwater streams of varying sizes that meander through the Everglades and finally mingle with the salt. This marriage forms what we call the "brackish edge of the backcountry." If you want a true wilderness experience, you should spend some time in these areas. Except for the occasional sound of a high-flying jet or a squawking heron, the silence can be deafening. This type of tranquility may not be for everyone, but if you enjoy watching birds such as egrets, ibis, spoonbills, ospreys and eagles, along with a few alligators, you'll love it.

You'll love it even more if you take a fly rod with you. A little exploring may be necessary, but it usually doesn't take very long to find some activity. Tarpon and snook are the main targets. Both are very adaptable as to the water types they can survive in. They're happy in everything that ranges from pure salt to slightly brackish water. The salinity of this swamp water can vary greatly, depending on the flow of the fresh water and the stage of the tide. In places that have higher percentages of fresh water, usually more upstream or where springs feed the river, you're likely to find largemouth bass too. Many times, we've caught all three species—tarpon, snook and bass—in the same area, sometimes within a few feet of each other.

The water can vary from brownish to crystal clear. The majority of the water has a characteristic swamp-stained, or coffee-colored, hue to it. About thirty miles east of Marco, there's a tiny river that's as clear as any spring creek you'll find in Montana and the bottom is lined with lush green vegetation. It's always fun to fish there, not only because of the beauty and solitude, but also because it's loaded with small snook, mostly one- to two-pounders. They're a real kick on a short 5-weight rod and a size #6 Madam X.

The rivers provide fishing all year long but are especially good during the winter. When cold fronts start dropping into Florida from the north, one after another, the nighttime low temperatures fall into the 40's and the daytime highs usually run in the low- to mid-70's. This is great weather for humans, but disaster for the fish. Forty-degree nights mean that the temperature of the shallow backwaters will be lucky to hit the mid-60's during the day. Fish like jacks and reds survive quite well and will keep on feeding but the more temperature-sensitive fish like snook and baby tarpon will vacate the cold flats in search of warmer water. Some of the snook will travel out into the open water and camp out in forty- to sixty-foot holes. The rest of the snook and the baby tarpon move up into the rivers where they'll be more comfortable in a very stable environment. Due to the springs that feed the rivers, the water temperature will fluctuate only a few degrees. This keeps the fish warmer in the winter and cooler in the summer. There are several other factors that make the environment of the river more stable than the environment of the shallow bays and flats. First of all, the rivers have a greater depth. The deeper the water the less the effect of the temperature of the air. Secondly, the percent of shade as compared to the total surface area of the water is much higher on a narrow river than a fifty-acre bay. This will help keep the water cooler in the summer. Also, the tides have far less effect the farther inland you go. This means that extreme low spring tides are not likely to run fish out of the rivers. Finally, the effects of the wind are minimized. In a large bay, a heavy wind can not only keep the tide from coming in but it also can rile up the water and make it very murky and muddy.

No matter how stable the environment and how great the comfort factor, food is the number one requirement of the fish, and the rivers fill the bill perfectly. The food supply in a river is more stable than most outside areas, where the fish pretty much rely on the tide to bring them their food. We've seined numerous rivers and found both the diversity and volume of "goodies" to be incredible. It's almost like seining a fertile trout stream. Instead of finding mayflies and caddisflies, we find numerous species of crabs, baitfish, and shrimp. You can generally tell how good the food supply is by looking at the fish you catch. River fish always look fat and healthy.

Typical cover in a
backcountry river

If you like to fish around cover, you'll be right at home on
a backcountry river, especially the small ones where you can
easily cast to both banks. The amount of cover is incredible. In
fact, part of the problem in fishing this type of water is decid-
ing where to throw next. All of it looks good; however, you
have to pick out what looks the very best and cover it efficiently. You need a system that will give you maximum coverage with a minimum number of casts. Too many anglers spend
too much time in one spot. These fish will normally hit on the
first cast, so unless you've had a "looker," it's silly to cover the
same area over and over. Keep in mind that the fisherman who
covers the most water during the day will almost always catch
the most fish. Coverage is the name of the game.

In most situations, tarpon and snook will move at least five
feet to take a fly, so if you make a cast every ten feet along the
shoreline, you've pretty well got things covered. If you can apply the techniques we discussed earlier, like using reach and

curve casts to get *parallel* retrieves, then you can *really* get maximum coverage with minimum effort. This, of course, allows you to move along at a faster pace. We also discussed how to identify edges that are the places where fish like to hang out. The problem with rivers is that there are too many edges; so many that it's hard to cover them all in a short period of time. What you must learn is how to recognize the very best edges. Target them as real hotspots and give them extra attention.

The key to identifying these places where fish like to hang out is observation. It sounds simple, but, like anything else, takes a little practice. Here's how to get started. First, learn to use your eyes like a zoom lens on a camera. Start with the wide-angle mode and scan the shoreline you're going to fish, looking for anything that stands out and grabs your attention. Your eyes will automatically gravitate to any irregularities such as an extra-large tree, a brush pile, a mangrove point, a deep, shaded pocket, or a small bay lined with exposed roots. This will give you a pretty good idea where you should be concentrating your efforts. As you start fishing, focus with your eyes in telephoto mode to determine precisely where to cast your fly. With a little experience you'll find that you'll quite often be able to predict where your next strike is coming from.

We use our backcountry skiffs to fish some of the larger rivers, but most of the time we use a small two-man rowboat. It only weighs eighty pounds, so we can throw it in the back of our pick-up and launch it anywhere. With a small electric motor and a set of oars, we can cover a lot of miles in a day of fishing. The Water Otter is the most efficient way of maneuvering in tight quarters and allows you to get incredibly close to the fish. It's a real stealth machine, but if you're squeamish about alligators, it might not be for you. Canoes are fine if only one person is fishing. One of the great features about this type of fishing is that you hardly ever see any other anglers. Also, you rarely have a problem with the wind since you're protected by the trees.

Speaking of tight quarters, we usually drop down to seven- or eight-foot rods when we fish the small rivers. There are times when six-footers would be better. Short, light rods are great for the casting, but you need strong leaders and tough shock tippets to handle big snook and baby tarpon in such places. We use leaders that are a little shorter than the rod. They have a twenty-pound breaking strength and a thirty-pound shock tippet. Set your drag at about four pounds.

The same flies that we use around the mangroves in the shallow bays work well in the rivers. However, we emphasize topwater flies a little more. The Fluter and regular soft-foam poppers are deadly. Tarpon will scare you to death when they explode on a popper at such close range. If you can handle the casting, the popper-dropper rig is the most effective of all. In tight areas where you're trying to get the popper as close as possible to the branches, it's pretty easy to forget about the dropper and it will occasionally tangle in the mangroves.

Most of the time we shy away from weedless flies mainly because they promote sloppy casting, but in tight quarters you might want to consider putting a mono loop on a few of your streamers and poppers. For Fluters and regular poppers, insert a U-shaped piece of twenty- to thirty-pound mono into the underside of the body on either side of the shank. Make the two holes with a dubbing needle and glue in with epoxy. Looking from the side, the loop should extend slightly lower than the point and just miss the hook when it's bent to the rear. To add to a streamer, use a match or lighter to melt a ball at each end of the U and figure-eight to the hook just behind the eye. This little loop makes a fly about as weedless as a fly can possibly be, yet is easy to attach.

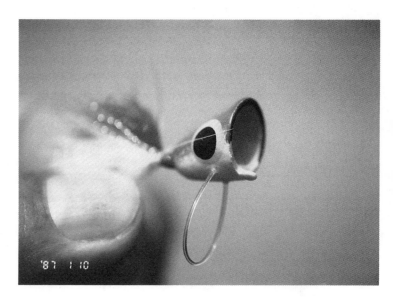

Regular popper with mono loop

We saved the bad news for last. Be sure to bring along bug juice for mosquitoes and no-see-ums.

MAN-MADE STRUCTURES

Man-made structures can't compete with the aesthetics of Mother Nature's back bays and rivers, but on occasion you can experience some incredible fishing around such places as canals, walls, docks, and bridges. In fact, one of the biggest snook we've ever seen took a crab pattern under a fifty-foot yacht moored in a canal near downtown Naples. After two dazzling jumps, Mr. Linesides ran off a hundred yards of backing and severed the leader when he swam under the dock on the other side of the canal. The largest jack crevalle ever caught by one of our students was hooked along a seawall in front of a marina and was finally landed a half-mile away in the shadow of the Marco Bridge. This brute calculated out at a little over fourteen pounds and took almost an hour to land on a 7-weight rod. These fish were not found in the most scenic part of the backcountry, but certainly provided some excitement.

There are literally thousands of miles of canals in the state of Florida; in the city of Naples alone, there are well over a hundred miles of them. These canals, all of which are somehow connected to the salt, produce some wonderful fishing and are tailor-made for the fly fisherman, especially a beginner. They are great places for the neophyte to cut his teeth on the sport and for individuals fishing on a budget to experience some relatively good fishing without breaking the bank.

You never know what you're going to catch in a canal. Along the Tamiami Trail and around Everglades City you have a good shot at tarpon and snook, while the canals in the Golden Gate area are more likely to produce bass and bluegills. Jacks, ladyfish, and snook show up frequently in the canals around Marco. A great way to spend a day is to go "canal hopping." In many areas, just walking the banks is fun and effective. However, there are places where you'll wish you had some type of small watercraft. The Water Otter is perfect for these places,

Canal with dock

but a canoe or small rowboat will suffice nicely. Poppers and streamers both work well, but poppers are more fun. A 7-weight rod is all the stick you'll need.

Canals provide an excellent alternative during the winter months when the shallow backwaters get cold. When the weather is exceptionally cold, the fishing may be better in the afternoon after the sun has warmed the water. With these conditions, fish a canal that runs east and west, concentrating your casts on the north bank. This is the old "sunny side of the street" trick and often works quite well. When the weather is warm, be sure to start early, at the crack of dawn if possible. Tarpon and snook are usually much more cooperative during the first hours of daylight. Keep your eyes peeled for rolling fish—they can be very subtle—and air bubbles on the surface that are signs that tarpon are below.

Some canals were built to connect major bodies of water, usually for the purpose of allowing boats to travel back and forth from one area to another. These can be terrific fisheries during the peak flow period of a spring tide. They are normally larger canals and are difficult to fish effectively from the bank. The best way to fish them is drifting with the current and pounding your fly as tightly to the bank as possible, making four or five quick strips and then repeating as fast as possible. The whole object is coverage. Try to hit the bank every five to ten feet. You must be quick with your delivery and adept with your hand dexterity. This routine separates the men from the boys. You've got to be a real "casting-retrieving machine" to get proper coverage. If the water is too deep, the current too fast, or both, you'll need some weight. Use a weighted fly or add weight to the leader. The simplest method is to slide a metal sleeve on your shock tippet before you tie the fly on with a loop knot. It can't come off, it's reusable, it's easy to cast and you don't have to worry about carrying both the weighted and un-weighted version of the same pattern.

Be sure you're fishing the right side of the canal, the side the fish are on. One side is always better than the other, with the contour of the bottom being the determining factor. Most of the fish will run down the side that has the sharpest, deepest drop-off. Even if the canal was dug out to be perfectly symmetrical, peak tidal flows will cut to one side or the other. Here's where a depth finder comes in handy. Also, watch the herons and egrets since they're not about to stand on the wrong side of the canal.

Anchoring up at the end is a little bit more boring than drifting the canal, but it can be very effective. The problem with this method is trying to figure out when the fish will pass by the boat during the cycle of the tide. You could, of course, anchor up and cast for the whole six hours but that really would get boring. We find that the fish normally come in quicker and go out later. In other words, for an incoming tide, you might set up one to two hours into the change and for an outgoing tide, anchor up about three to four hours after the tide peaks. You could use this information as a starting point and then keep experimenting. Make accurate notes of everything, including variables such as wind velocity, wind direction, how long the wind was blowing and barometric pressure. With enough information and experimentation you should be able to predict, with pretty good accuracy, when the fish will show.

The best place to anchor is normally at the "downstream" end of a canal. This is where the funnel system opens up and allows the fish to hold comfortably while they pick off the goodies that are drifting by. Fish are less likely to be at the "upstream" end of the canal because of the difficulty of holding in the fast water. When it comes to eating, fish will always feed where they can get the most food with the least effort.

Over half of the large jacks we've caught have been taken off the concrete seawalls that are found in front of condos, marinas and private residences. By large, we mean fish in the ten- to fifteen-pound category. Jacks in this size-range are absolute brutes. Pound for pound, they fight as hard and as long as anything that swims in the ocean. They are responsible for more broken rods than any other species. Although jacks are the predominant target when fishing the walls, we also catch redfish, ladyfish, snapper, trout, and snook—sometimes very large ones.

The very best time to fish along these concrete barriers is at the crack of dawn during maximum tidal flow. It doesn't seem to matter much if the current is incoming or outgoing. The main requirements are good tide and poor light. Even if the tide is not a real banger, it pays to check out the walls just before the sun comes over the horizon. Once the fishing slows, usually after an hour or so of daylight, it's time to head for the mangroves. Evenings can be good, but are not nearly as consistent as early morning.

"Wall banging" is not only easy but can be very exciting, especially when topwater patterns are used. The surface smash of a ten-pound jack is phenomenal. Quite often they'll make several passes before they connect. This is where you have to really concentrate on keeping your rod tip down. It's terribly frustrating to miss the biggest fish of the day because you reacted too quickly and jerked the fly away. Be patient and let him "eat it" before you set the hook. The walls are excellent places for the beginning fly fisherman to gain experience. The casting is about as easy as it gets and when the fish are in, you're pretty much assured of some action.

The reason the walls are so good is that they form one of the best edges of all. They are very similar to the steep or undercut banks of a trout stream. The layer of current running tight to the wall is slowed by friction, thus forming a very comfortable zone where the fish can hold. The faster current, a foot or so out from the wall, brings the food conveyor belt-style right past the fishes' noses. It's the same old story: fish love to be in the best possible position so they can grab the most food with the least amount of effort. With this in mind, it becomes obvious that the fly should be presented tight to the wall, certainly within a foot or two. Most of the time, casts are made perpendicularly to the face of the wall. If the boat is moving slowly enough, you'll probably get plenty of coverage. However, if you can make your fly swim parallel to the wall through the use of reach casts and mending, you can cover all of the best holding water. This technique will, in turn, allow you to move the boat faster, covering even more water.

The flies we use for wall banging are pretty much the same ones we use for fishing mangroves, bays and rivers. Shrimpys, Sea Devils and Fluters all do a great job. However, there are times when a noisy soft-foam popper is preferred over everything else. Use one with a large cupped face that really makes a big commotion when you pop your wrist on the retrieve. Sometimes we'll use a hookless popper to attract fish for beginning students in our schools. You can really get a big jack mad when you yank a fly out of his mouth two or three times in the same retrieve. Teasers not only work well on the walls but can be dynamite in the mangroves. You can throw it way back in the branches and heavy cover without getting hung up.

Docks can be real hotspots because they provide the overhead cover and shade that many fish prefer. Snook, much like largemouth bass, love to ambush their victims, so they spend a great deal of time in the shadows planning their next attack. To cover a dock properly, you should make parallel casts along each side and also fire several tight loops underneath to get your fly back into the shade as far as possible. If the water is three or more feet deep, you'll want to let the fly settle to the bottom a few times before starting the retrieve. Docks can present a problem when the tide is zipping through at high speed. With the fish both under and strung out on the downstream side, you must be very careful that the strong current doesn't sweep your fly into a piling. One trick is to throw a curve that hooks your fly under the dock from an upstream angle. Then mend more line directly upstream from the fly. This should hold it in a good fish-taking position for a few seconds. However, if a fish takes, you may have a problem guiding him out of the pilings. Of course, this is a better problem to have than

Row of docks

no hook-up at all. The other method is to position the boat directly below the dock, on the downstream side, and throw a supertight loop that puts your fly well under the dock. This is not the best presentation angle but it often works. Sometimes a popper will do the job.

Another approach is to use one of the backward-swimming flies. They're a little tough to control in strong tides, but work well when the current is slow. The best method of presentation is to throw a slack-line cast that drops the fly to the edge of the dock and then quickly feed more loose line. This keeps the line and leader from putting tension on the fly, allowing it to drop backwards with a free, natural motion.

Jetties are pier-shaped structures that are made from rocks and boulders. They are fished the same way you'd fish a wall, except there are two sides to a jetty. Sometimes the biggest problem is finding out which side to fish. Factors such as tide, wind direction and depth usually determine where the fish are. Rocks are a little less forgiving than smooth concrete so you'll want to carry a few bendbacks and flies with weedguards.

Abutments and other support structure associated with bridges can offer some excellent angling opportunities. They provide shade, protection from heavy tidal flows and a great

Bridge abutment and structure

place for fish to lie in wait to intercept drifting shrimp, crabs and baitfish. Fishing these areas is basically a matter of anchoring and covering the structure as thoroughly as possible. The problem you'll face there is getting good *vertical* coverage. For all the other types of fishing we've discussed, it was a matter of *horizontal* coverage, trying to effectively cast and retrieve over as many square feet of the water's surface as possible. Getting your fly down to where the fish are is critical to your success around bridge abutments and related structure. Fast-sinking lines or extra-long leaders with metal sleeves will be necessary. A good time to experiment with this type of fishing is at low tide, for several reasons. Lower water level and minimal current flow make it a lot easier to fish deep, and fish that must leave the shallow bays at low tide will head straight for the deeper water around bridges.

7

Tackle and Other Tools of the Trade

INTRODUCTION

The backcountry is a whole new ballgame for the typical trout and bass fisherman from the North. There are many more species to be caught, sometimes as many as seven or eight in one day. You never know if you're going to hook a tiny half-pound snapper or a tarpon over a hundred pounds. Pound for pound, saltwater fish fight much harder than their freshwater counterparts—and, with their supercharged metabolism, swim two to three times faster. In the salt, there's always someone bigger and faster than you are, so you have to be quick. It's strictly survival of the fittest!

With these facts in mind, the backcountry angler needs to have equipment that can survive the faster, more powerful runs of ocean-going fish. Rods must be stronger, reels must have silky smooth drags, leaders must be heavier, and knots must be tied with great precision. In addition, numerous other tools of the trade must be considered.

RODS, REELS,
AND LINES

Fly rods have gone through quite an evolution over the past ten years. As we develop plastics with higher and higher strength-to-weight ratios, mainly for the aerospace industry, rods get better and better. With present-day models, the average angler can cast tighter loops and develop greater line control than ever before, and most important, all of this can be accomplished with very little effort. For backcountry fishing, this "lightness factor" is critical. Pounding the mangroves is undoubtedly one of the most demanding types of fly fishing there is, although steelheading might rival it for pure energy required. To be successful at both you must turn into a casting-retrieving machine. However, much more accuracy is needed to handle the masses of tight cover found in the backcountry. A full day of casting can become quite a physical chore with a rod that is too heavy and cumbersome.

The most popular rod length for this type of fishing is the nine-footer, although shorter rods, down to seven-and-a-half feet, have recently found their way into our arsenal. Remember, an eight-footer is not only lighter and tends to throw narrower loops, but is also a more efficient tool for fighting and landing fish. In really tight mangrove situations, a tiny seven-and-a-half-foot stick is pure delight. Rods longer than nine feet obviously are a little heavier and seem more unwieldy. In the final analysis rod length should be determined by your personal preference. Use a rod that "feels" right and is enjoyable to fish with. Rods that handle 7-, 8-, or 9-weight lines are best for most backcountry fishing, with the nine-foot-#8 outfit being the most popular. There are exceptions, of course. We usually carry #10 to #12 rigs in the boat when we plan on encountering large tarpon, eighty pounds and over, and almost always carry a #6 system for fish like small snook and tiny baby tarpon.

It's difficult to say how much improvement we'll see in rod-blank design in the future; however, considering the progress made by the major rod companies over recent years, we assume there will be steady progress in both action and weight reduction. This will undoubtedly come about through the development of new materials and the upgrading of specifications on present ones. Other areas of rod design, especially guides and handles, certainly need to be improved. One of the major problems in shooting a flyline is the friction caused by the tip-top. With the standard "pear-shaped" design on present-day fly rods, the final forward shoot of the delivery cast is greatly inhibited due to the dramatic build-up of friction. This resistance is magnified when the flyline is squeezed down into the small end of the pear on the frontcast. When this happens, much more surface friction is created than when the line is rubbing the large side of the pear on the backcast. You can easily check out this phenomenon by rotating your rod into various positions as you cast. We've experimented with other tip-top shapes and found that more rounded guides create less friction and shoot better than the conventional pear type.

Another improvement would be a handle material that is soft, comfortable, and easy to grip. When you're casting all day long with a big rod, your hands really take a beating. With a conventional cork handle, it takes a lot of fishing time to get in shape, and most anglers simply don't log that many hours. As a result, we recommend using a glove on the casting hand to avoid sore spots and blisters. Recently, however, we've had the opportunity to test some rods with soft handles and have been very impressed with their softness, comfort and, most important, how easy they are on your hands. While on the subject of handles, be sure to have one that fits your hand properly. It is our observation that many anglers are struggling with handles that are too big. Not only are oversized handles uncomfortable, but they cause fatigue and adversely affect your casting stroke. It's obvious that the rod manufacturers try to fit the largest hands. It's harder to add on than take off, so many men and most all women and children end up with diameters that are much too large. The remedy is to sand the cork down to size. This can easily be done by hand and takes about twenty to thirty minutes. Someday, much like golf clubs and tennis racquets, we'll be able to order the exact style and size handle we want. A final note on handles. Some rods come with fighting grips. However, unless you're an experienced angler, you're probably better off without one. Reaching up the blank that far with the rod at the wrong angle can greatly overload the tip and cause the rod to break.

As mentioned earlier, one of the most important features of modern-day graphite fly rods are their extreme lightness. In order to achieve this featherlike feel, wall thicknesses are very thin, which in turn creates rods that are quite susceptible to breakage. Over the past few years, between the two of us we've averaged about five or six broken rods per year. The rod companies are very good about repairing and replacing them, but it can be quite an inconvenience if you only take one rod on a trip. Always take an extra rod or two. It's a good idea to carry a travel rod in your suitcase.

Finally, be sure you rinse your rod in fresh water after a trip to the salt. Give extra attention to the reel seat parts and guides, especially where the feet of the guide make contact with the rod. You can use an old toothbrush to better clean these critical areas. An occasional wipe with furniture polish is not a bad idea either.

When it comes to fly reels, our advice is to buy the best you can afford. For freshwater trout fishing, reels aren't all that important. However, when it comes to fishing in the backcountry you'll want to consider three main features: capacity, drag and weight. Saltwater species make much longer and stronger runs than their freshwater counterparts so it is advisable to have a reel that holds at least 150 yards of backing. If you're fishing mainly for tarpon it would be better to have 200 to 250 yards. Usually, in the spring when we chase larger tarpon, we carry a special rig anyway. Even though some of our biggest fish, tarpon up to 140 pounds, have been caught on relatively inexpensive palming reels, the old System 10s and 11s, it's nice to have one of the more modern models with a silky smooth drag. The weight of the reel is not much of a factor when you're sight fishing for tarpon. You really aren't doing a lot of casting in these situations. When you're fishing a 7-weight outfit all day in the mangroves, it's a different story. You're literally making hundreds of casts to cover the water thoroughly. A lightweight reel makes life a lot more bearable under these conditions. At the end of the day, rinse it with fresh water, clean, and oil. Spray WD-40 or equivalent on the reel foot and on the threads of the reel seat; then wipe down with a light coat of oil.

Anglers who fish with us for the first time are usually quite surprised when they see how shallow the water is. In fact, we jokingly tell them when they first get in our skiff, "If you fall out of the boat, don't drown. Just stand up." At least three-quarters of the time we're fishing water that's only one to three feet deep, so we rarely have need for any type of sinking lines. Most of our angling is done with floating, weight-forward, saltwater taper. There are several specialty tapers on the market, such as bonefish and tarpon, and they do the job, but our favorite is the standard saltwater variety. There is certainly a need for a special backcountry taper and we feel that the line manufacturers will address this problem in the near future. In the meantime, we hand-make our own tapers by cutting up either standard saltwater tapers or regular weight-forward lines and putting them back together to create an extremely short head. Almost all present-day weight-forward lines are designed with a drop-off point, where the belly ends, that is thirty or more feet from the tip of the line. In order to take full advantage of this design and get maximum shootability, the caster must start with at least thirty-five feet of line past the tip of the rod. With a ten-foot leader, that means when the fly is approximately forty-five feet from the boat, it's time to make the pickup and shoot back out to sixty or sixty-five feet. We normally want to strip the fly so that it covers at least fifteen to twenty feet of water. This is a tough job for any novice or intermediate caster! In fact, it is our observation that less than twenty percent of all fly fishermen can handle this situation. We know, because we see it all the time in our schools and charters.

Another factor that makes this situation even more difficult is that a lot of mangrove fishing is done in very close quarters. Sometimes you only throw twenty feet of line and strip the fly right up to the boat. For these close-in casts, and to help reduce false casts, we make up lines with very short bellies that start tapering down approximately fifteen feet from the tip. This pushes the center of gravity well forward and increases the "moment arm" effect. These little "heads" not only help the beginner to expand the amount of water covered and reduce false casting, but also help the better casters to increase their efficiency, especially in windy situations.

When it comes to color, pick one you like. The fish in the backcountry really don't care what color your line is. Bright lines don't normally scare fish, but bad casting does. It boils down to the fact that you should pick a color that gives you the most mental confidence, which of course is an important factor in anything you do. Some anglers like the high-visibility colors so they can see exactly what's happening with their line in the air and on the water. It's difficult to correct casting mistakes if you can't see what the line is doing as it rolls through the air and how it is lying on the water. Other anglers feel that bright lines definitely scare fish so they should use one that's less visible. If you don't know which way to go, you can compromise by purchasing a high-visibility line and then either dyeing or marking the first ten feet with a more somber color.

Occasionally, but not very often, you might encounter a need for some type of sinking line. There are a few tarpon holes, for example, that drop to a depth of ten to fifteen feet where a fast-sinking line, either full or sink tip, might come in handy. The most effective method, however, is to lengthen the leader, sometimes up to twenty feet, and slide a lead sleeve over the shock tippet. Nothing sinks faster than mono with lead on it. Another place where a sinking line can be used effectively is along a very steep drop-off, like the bank of a canal, a wall or any deep cut. Use a weedless fly, such as a heavily dressed bendback or a keel fly, on a short leader and cast across the deep water, allowing the line to sink to the bottom. When you retrieve, the fly will follow the contour of the bottom. A line that is sometimes deadly when fished over the grass beds is a uniform sink line. By using a neutral-density fly, you can let the whole system sink until it's just above the tips of the turtle grass and then retrieve.

The sun and the salt play havoc with your fly line, so you must learn to give it lots of tender, loving care. We feel ecstatic if we get two months' usage out of a line. Of course, that's based on using them almost every day for several hours or more. The sun leaches out flexibility and the salt abrades your line like a piece of sandpaper. To counteract these elements, you must rinse the line with fresh water after every trip, even if you only fished for a few minutes. It is best to wipe the line dry—stripping it out on the lawn and running a paper towel or cloth down its length will do. Then use a line cleaner and polish. All of this will take only ten minutes and will be well worth the effort. To get rid of kinks and twists, drag the line, without the fly, behind the boat or hold it in a fast tide.

LEADERS AND
KNOTS

Over the years, much emphasis has been put on the fact that in order to be a saltwater fly fisherman, you must be able to construct complicated leaders with fancy knots. This is probably one of the reasons there are so few anglers on the flats and in the backcountry. Many simply got scared off trying to figure out how to assemble a typical saltwater leader. The main reason for learning Bimini twists, spider hitches, Duncan loops and all of the other knots is to be able to qualify for a world record. If that's what you're interested in, then you'll have to go ahead and learn the knots. We just like to have fun fishing and don't get too excited about a record catch. In fact, a couple of years ago, we were fishing with Tom Smith, a good friend of ours from Michigan, when he hooked and landed a gigantic snook in the 10,000 Islands. We took a few pictures, measured the length and girth and then gently released the huge linesider. Using the formula for calculating weight, we found out the fish was well over forty pounds, about twelve pounds above the present world record on a fly. Our excitement was the thrill of seeing such a magnificent fish and the enjoyment of spending a beautiful day in the backcountry.

Here's the formula for a leader that's simple to tie, yet performs very well in the mangroves. Since most rods are nine-footers, we keep the leader about eight feet long so that the line-to-leader connection doesn't cause a problem going back and forth through the tip-top.

	Length	Material
Butt	5′	30# mono
Taper	1½′	20# mono
Shock Tippet	1½′	30# mono

You can make changes to suit your specific needs. For example, if you want a lighter breaking strength, say fifteen-pound test, just change the taper from eighteen inches of twenty-pound test to ten inches of twenty-pound test followed by eight inches of fifteen-pound test. Substitute twelve-pound test for the fifteen if you want to go even lighter. Don't go too light, however, or you'll be losing lots of flies in the trees. When you break off, you rarely get your fly back, as it almost always drops in the water.

Another substitute you might want to try is using thirty-pound flat mono for the five-foot butt section. The flat monofilament throws a tighter loop and turns over like a rocket. For a really light outfit, like a 5-weight or 6-weight rod, and small flies, six-and-a-half feet of twenty-pound flat mono followed by one-and-a-half feet of thirty-pound regular mono make a terrific leader.

Another option is to use two strands of fifteen- or twenty-pound mono for the shock tippet. This setup replaces wire and often saves the day when you encounter toothy critters like barracuda or schools of mackerel. We've used this system many times in Alaska when fishing for northern pike. Quite often one strand of mono will get cut by a tooth, but rarely two.

If you're going for tarpon over twenty pounds, you'll want to beef your shock tippet up to forty-pound test; from forty to sixty pounds, jump to sixty-pound test; and for fish any bigger, go to eighty-pound mono. Also, if you're using a rod in the 10-to-12 weight category you might want to use a forty-pound butt section.

There are only three knots that you need to know: the nail knot, the surgeons knot and loop knot. Two others are valuable but not absolutely necessary: the blood knot and the Albright.

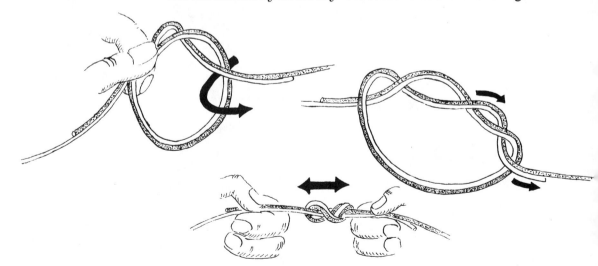

The *surgeons knot* is used to join two strands of monofilament.

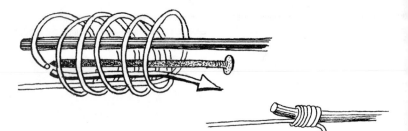

The *nail knot* is used to attach the leader to the fly line and also the Dacron backing to the fly line.

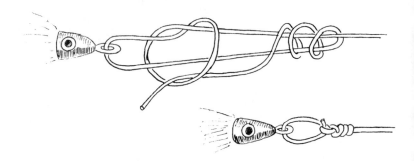

The *loop knot* is used to attach the fly to the shock tippet.

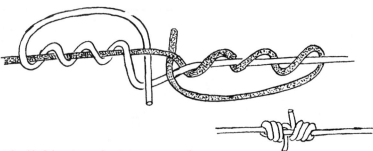

The *blood knot* is used to join two strands of monofilament of similar size.

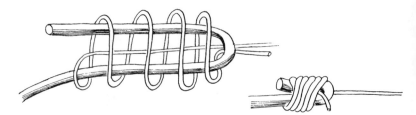

The *Albright knot* is used to join two strands of monofilament that vary greatly in size, for example, fifteen-pound test to forty-pound.

BACKCOUNTRY
BOATS

You really don't need a twenty-thousand-dollar skiff to fish the backcountry, although we have to admit that it's awfully nice to have one. The main requirement is that you are equipped to handle shallow water. Most backcountry angling takes place in depths of one to three feet, so your boat should draw no more than 12 to 15 inches of water when it's on plane and properly trimmed. For ease of poling and maneuvering with an electric motor, it should be well balanced so that it sits level on the water. An unbalanced boat is difficult to control and tends to spin in the wind. A hull weighing over 900 pounds, especially when it's powered with a gigantic motor, makes a poor choice. The most popular watercraft for fishing the shallow backcountry is the "flats" boat, and there are many models to choose from. Far less popular are the boats that are so common with the thousands of bass fishermen across the country; however, don't sell these "bass" boats short. Certain models are excellent for fishing the backcountry. There are advantages and disadvantages to both. Flat boats have cleaner or more "trouble-free" casting areas and are easier to pole. Some bass boats, especially the aluminum ones, are so light they'll go almost anywhere, and most have carpeted decks which provide a much better surface for large coils of fly line.

For the fly fisherman, one of the biggest problems you face when casting from any boat are all of the obstructions that seem to come out of nowhere to tangle your line. There are cleats, motors, brackets, handles, steering wheels, foot controls, ice chests, and seat backs, not to mention the items on your own person: buttons, buckles, shoelaces, trouser bottoms, and even your own feet. You must make every effort to keep your line clear. Tangles always seem to happen on the most important casts.

Cleats not only snag your fly line, but are responsible for many broken rods. If you don't have the "pop-up" cleats, tape them or cover them with one of those insulated jackets that keep cans of soda cold. A piece of netting with a few lead sinkers strategically attached works great for covering obstructions. Wetted-down beach towels and blankets work well

Tangles on boat

too. Silver carpet tape can be used to cover many small objects including your shoelaces and trouser bottoms. Another aid in clearing line in the boat or on a dock is a plastic pail with some sand or other weight in the bottom to keep it stationary.

If you feel you need an elevated casting platform, you can lash a large cooler to the deck with quick-pull straps or bungee cords. Cement a piece of indoor-outdoor carpeting on top for a comfortable, nonslip surface. Poling platforms are an option you might want to consider but they're not as important in the backcountry as they would be on the clearwater flats of the Keys and Bahamas. They're impractical if you fish by yourself most of the time.

Most modern backcountry boats are equipped with an electric motor; in fact, it's a must if you're going to cover the water efficiently. A foot control is also mandatory to keep your hands free for casting.

You should always carry a chart of the area you are fishing. Back in the mangroves, everything looks the same, especially at high tide. Study the chart thoroughly before you fish a new area and you may save yourself from getting lost and spending the night in "mosquito heaven." Charts basically tell you where *not* to go and will help you avoid dangers such as oyster bars and rocky shoals. Charts can help you locate good fishing spots if you interpret the information properly. For example, if you see that there's a ten-foot hole in the middle of an area that's only two feet deep, there's an excellent chance that hole will be full of fish at low tide. Likewise, a narrow pass that shows up on the chart to be the *only* entrance to a large system of bays and backwaters should be dynamite during maximum tidal flow. To find the time of maximum flow, you then look at your tide atlas, which should also be carried in the boat.

The tide atlas gives you a wealth of valuable information. It tells you the times that high and low tides will occur, how high and how low each will be, the time and direction of maximum flow and how strong each tide will be. Remember to correct these times to your specific area and that the tides are affected by such variables as barometric pressure and the wind: how hard it blows, how long it blows and what direction it's coming from.

If you become a boat owner, there are a number of items that the U.S. Coast Guard will require you to have aboard, such as first-aid kit, fire extinguisher, flares, life vests, throwable flotation device, paddle, flashlight, whistle, horn, and anchor.

Other items, besides your fishing gear, that you might want to consider: compass, tool kit, shear pins, fuses, jumper cables, matches, cigarette lighter, gloves, insect repellent, hook remover, toilet paper, paper towels, extra anchor, release buoy, raingear, and depth finder.

HOW TO FISH ON A BUDGET

If you aren't ready to buy your own backcountry skiff and you can't afford a guide every day, although it's advisable to go with one a few times to learn the ropes, there are several alternatives. First of all, it's possible to simply go wading and do fairly well. You can wade the outside beaches, passes, mangrove flats, along canals and around bridges. Some of the biggest snook and jacks have been taken on the main beaches. You never know what's going to swim by. This can be a very demanding type of fishing. Try to get the wind in the most favorable position, if possible, and then methodically work right or left trying to cover the water as efficiently as possible. Most of the time, the Gulf water is extremely clear, giving the fish great visibility. They'll move ten feet or more to take your fly, so unless you've had a "looker," make your casts at least twenty feet apart. You'll find this is a pretty rapid pace, allowing you to cover a mile or more of beach in a relatively short time. Long lazy casts followed by stripping that swims the fly most of the way in are the name of the game. Don't wade out more than knee-deep, as many of the strikes will come within twenty to thirty feet of shore. The longer the cast, the better the coverage. Try to pick up and shoot right back without false casting. Force yourself to do it this way and you'll not only cover more water in less time but you'll quickly improve your shooting. Neoprene booties or similar footgear is recommended as there can be stingrays in the area. Be sure to wear a hat, put on lots of sunblock and take a few extra flies and tippet material. Fanny packs are fine for the extra gear; however, a small piece of foam, either flat or ripple, tied around the neck with a piece of mono is lighter and easier. Your nippers and small spool of tippet material can be threaded on the mono. This type of fishing can be a lot of fun. If you get tired, you can take a swim, lie in the sun or look for shells.

You can do the same type of fishing along the outer passes and around bridges. The best time is during a medium-to-heavy tidal flow. You don't have to walk very far because the fish will be passing through. Concentrate your efforts on the "downstream" side of the pass or bridge. Spring tides can really rip through these areas, so be cautious of strong currents.

Wading the mangrove flats can be a little tricky. Some are firm and can be waded easily, while others are so soft and mushy you sink up to your knees on every step. You have to do some experimenting to determine the good ones from the bad. Definitely wear protective footgear for this type of fishing. The best time to wade the mangroves would be at maximum tidal flow during a falling spring tide, which would be about an hour and a half to two hours after dead-high tide.

Canals can provide some of the most exciting fishing of all. In this type of fishing, you do very little wading. Instead, you walk the bank and look for visible signs that tarpon are present. These are usually small fish, in the five-to-ten-pound range, and often reveal their location by rolling or releasing air that forms bubbles at the surface. If no fish are showing, then you get some wonderful surprises by blind casting. You never know what is going to hit: tarpon, snook, ladyfish, jack crevalle, or a largemouth bass! If you fish on the surface, it's even more exciting. There's nothing like the explosion of a baby tarpon or large snook when they strike a topwater fly. Soft foam poppers are deadly for this type of fishing. Quite often we drop down to six-weight outfits, especially when we're into a lot of five-pound tarpon. Don't forget to bring plenty of insect repellent.

One of our best friends comes down from Pennsylvania every year and stays for a month. He attended one of our two-day schools and really got the bug for this kind of fishing. Even though he doesn't have a boat, he fishes the canals every morning and has a ball. Rare is the day that he doesn't have at least one hook-up with a baby tarpon. Along with the tarpon, he releases lots of snook and jack crevalle, most of which are hooked on poppers. By coming down in the off season, either before December or after April, his expenses are kept to a minimum.

For those of you who want to do more than just wade the beaches and walk the canals, there are a number of possibilities to consider. Here is a list of the various watercraft we've experimented with followed by the advantages and disadvantages of each:

1. **Float Tube** In 1972, we tried float tubes in the Keys. At low tide, we'd tie them to our waist and drag them along as we fished. There simply isn't enough water to fish out of them when the depth is less than three feet. At high tide, they were great for barracuda on the flats. In the backcountry, they are usable during extremely high tides and in deeper cuts and channels.

2. **Water Wagon** The water wagon is a small boat, six feet long, four feet wide and ten inches thick that weighs only twenty pounds. It is molded out of foam, propelled with scuba fins and is a big step up from a float tube. We started using it on the flats in the late seventies. It's a great little craft for fishing the backcountry since it can be maneuvered in water only a foot deep. The bad news is that it isn't made anymore.

3. **Inflatable Raft** These boats are like the ones used to float down Western rivers. We brought one down to Naples about ten years ago and it worked very well in the backcountry with a five-horsepower motor and a set of oars.

4. **Canoe** If you want to cover lots of water and cover it quietly, the canoe is excellent. We see more and more of them each year. The biggest problem is being confined to the sitting position for long periods of time.

5. **Water Otter** This is the latest version of the tiny one-man boats. It consists of two inflatable pontoons with a miniature rafting frame over the top. It can be powered by scuba fins, electric motor, gasoline motor, or oars. Fishing on the Otter is a real kick. It weighs about twenty-five pounds, draws only four inches of water and goes like a rocket when the oars are used. Fine-tuning with the flippers keeps you in perfect fishing position as you glide along the mangroves. You can get closer to the fish with the Water Otter than by any other method. If you learn to "ride the tide," you can cover ten or more miles in a day. The object is to ride an incoming tide and fish your way inland until the tide peaks, then fish back to your vehicle. We've caught tarpon over forty pounds fishing on the Otter.

Angler in Water Otter
fishing backcountry

6. ***Rowboat*** We also have a little two-man plastic rowboat that's great for going way back in the mangroves. It weighs about eighty pounds and will go all day long with an electric motor. It's very comfortable and has a flat bottom so you can easily stand up to cast. If the battery runs out, there's a set of oars to bring you home.

As you can see, there are many ways to fish the backcountry. To get started, even if you're on a budget, probably the best thing you can do is come down to the 10,000 Islands area and hire a guide for a couple of days, or better yet, attend a school. With a day of schooling and a day on the water, you'll learn all you need to know to get started—and we guarantee you'll be hooked.

Seasonal Movements of Backcountry Gamefish — and Angling Opportunities

Every angler who has ever taken a trip to a faraway location and experienced disappointment knows some weeks are better than others for whatever species you are hunting. The same is true for backcountry fly fishing. If you are planning a trip specifically for tarpon, bonefish, or snook, you will want to pick the very best time when the most fish are present and most active. If, however, you are going on a family vacation where backcountry exists and it is not the ideal month for tarpon, do not despair. Opportunity for exciting fly fishing for many species of gamefish will be present no matter what month you arrive.

The movements and feeding of backcountry fish, like all other fish, are determined by water temperature that, in the long term, is determined by the changing seasons. Weather fronts, barometric pressure, and spawning migrations will modify short-term conditions, but water temperature is the overriding factor. If we have knowledge of all of these factors we can adjust our tactics to the existing conditions with a reasonable chance of success, no matter which season we fish.

The farther away from the equator we fish, the greater the seasonal variation in the water temperature. Some saltwater fisheries very close to the equator, such as near Christmas Island, have very little fluctuation. The farther north or south, the greater the fluctuation. Obviously, in the Southern Hemisphere, the seasons will be reversed. We will give examples of areas close to 24° to 26°N latitude. This area includes Naples down to the Florida Keys on the Gulf of Mexico, the Keys north to Key Biscayne, and the Bahamas on the Atlantic side. If you are fishing farther north, say the South Carolina or Texas coast, you will have to compensate for the later spring and earlier fall dates.

The six major fly targets in the backcountry are snook, tarpon, redfish, spotted sea trout, bonefish, and permit, but many other species are present, either all year or seasonally. Most can be caught from just off the outside islands and passes to the extreme inside bays. Some, like bluefish, are seasonal, moving south in the fall, staying around all winter and then moving north in the spring. Sharks are around all the time, but the best backcountry fishing for sharks is in the warm months. Barracuda are a great winter fish in the Florida Keys. Cobia migrate south in the winter and can sometimes be found on shallow grass flats. The list goes on and on and each location is a little bit different. Local bait shops are a great help in tracking down these fish of opportunity.

Traditionally the first hint of spring at latitude 24° to 26°N is in March. We will start there and take it month by month, listing the seasonal movements of the six most important targets with a few references to special situations.

MARCH

March is a transitional month at these latitudes and can be as unpredictable as it is windy. On the other hand, if the weather cooperates, it can also be the beginning of the most spectacular fishing of the year. One day the fish are in the warm feeder streams and on the outside deep waters; the next day they are inside the barrier islands in the shallow bays and channels. March can be a mystery, but solve it and you will be raising big sea trout and lunker snook, or jumping giant tarpon coming inshore from their deep-water wintering areas.

MARCH SNOOK

If you are snook hunting, unless the weather is unseasonably warm, you will find them far inside, up the rivers and in creek mouths which fish best on the outgoing tides. In early spring, snook love mullet, so an imitation of a finger mullet is a good bet. If the water is above 70°, snook will begin to move outside the rivers and creeks. They can be found anywhere from the inside bays to the outside beaches. When the spring shrimp migration begins, everything will feed on them.

MARCH TARPON

Tarpon will begin coming in from their deep-water wintering areas, and by the third or fourth week of March they will be around. The really big ones, 100 pounds or more, will be off the outside islands. The smaller resident fish will be in the same areas you find snook, depending on weather. Small mud crabs and shrimp imitations are best for these backcountry fish.

MARCH REDFISH

In March, reds will be feeding in deep inside bays and up coastal rivers. Look for warm water and use baby mullet, crabs, and shrimp patterns.

MARCH SEA TROUT

March is the beginning of the spotted sea trout migration. From warmer offshore water and the inshore rivers and holes, they will move to the inside grassy flats. During the first two weeks in March, fish will be in the backcountry around mangrove islands, cuts, and oyster bars. A little later the focus is on the grassy flats, where really big specimens gather for the spring spawn. Shrimp and finger-mullet imitations are top producers. Any outside grassy flats are productive as well as the flats inside the barrier islands from Florida Bay around the Gulf shore to Texas and the estuaries on the east coast to North Carolina. Of course, the farther north you fish the later the inshore movement.

MARCH BONEFISH

Bonefish will move on the Atlantic-side flats from Biscayne Bay to Key West. March is also the beginning of the best fishing in the Bahamas. Shrimp imitations are a great producer as are small blue crabs and green reef crabs.

MARCH PERMIT

This is your best time to hook a large permit on a fly. And the lower Florida Keys are the best place to do it if the wind is not too strong. A medium-size blue crab imitation is tops.

MARCH SHEEPSHEAD

Sheepshead are usually considered a winter fish, but March is one of the best times to find tailing fish on shallow inshore flats and oyster bars from Marco Island north to the Florida panhandle. This is just like traditional bonefishing farther south except sheepshead are as finicky as permit. Small mud crab imitations are best.

APRIL

April is a continuation of late March fishing except it's much more reliable, less windy, and the fish are found in more shallow water as the warming trend continues.

APRIL SNOOK

April sees snook moving out of the coastal rivers and warm holes of winter; they now can be found all through the backcountry bays, cuts, and passes. Needlefish imitations are especially good this month, but the spring run of scaled sardines is starting. When you run into a school of these preferred baitfish, a good imitation is necessary. Also, the finger mullet, as always, is reliable.

APRIL TARPON

Tarpon become a dependable target in April when giants begin to move toward the Homosassa and Boca Grande areas. When water temperatures hit 75°, look for the big fish of spring. In Belize, April to June is the time for big tarpon to take flies in the mangrove bays and estuaries. The smaller fish from ten to fifty pounds are all over the Florida backcountry and are feeding. Use a ladyfish pattern for the big fish and small shrimp for the smaller ones.

APRIL REDFISH

The annual redfish migration is in full swing on the Atlantic side where offshore schools move to the Georgia and Carolina shores. They show up in Chesapeake Bay in May where they remain until October and early November. In the Florida backcountry, resident reds are now prowling the shallow flats in search of crabs and shrimp, and sight fishing comes into its own.

APRIL SEA TROUT

This is prime time to find the largest of these spotted beauties on the shallow, grassy flats and inside bays. Charlotte Harbor is probably the best in Florida, but Sarasota Bay runs a close second. From Florida Bay to Texas this is the fly fisher's best chance of a really big trout in skinny water. Practically any good imitation, from streamers and popping bugs to shrimp and crabs fished deep, will be successful.

APRIL BONEFISH AND PERMIT

Permit and bones will be tailing on warm days, especially on flats with an incoming tide from Key West to Biscayne Bay. Small crab and shrimp flies will be top producers, especially snapping shrimp.

MAY

This is the month it all comes together. It will be your best chance to score a grand slam (tarpon, reds, and snook) in the 10,000 Islands, or a supergrand slam (bonefish, tarpon, reds, permit, and snook) in Florida Bay. In a word, fishing *sizzles*! If you northern trout fishermen can forgo the Hendrickson hatches on the Eastern streams, May in the Florida backcountry will be well worth it. This month, there are fish everywhere in these latitudes. The water has warmed up and all of our target gamesters are feeding. So many species are active, it's difficult to choose which to hunt.

Redfish caught in
10,000 Islands

Sharon Chaffin with a tarpon

MAY SNOOK

Snook are gathering in big numbers around the passes all over Florida. They are in their pre-spawn feeding mode and the very best fishing is at night on outgoing tides. On the incoming tides they feed just off the outside beaches in the surf close to the passes and in the big outside bays. After spawning starts, usually around the full moon, the best fishing is in the morning as snook do not spawn in the daytime. This is great sight fishing. They are feeding on grunts, croakers, baby catfish, sand perch, and pinfish, but scaled sardines, which are now showing up in huge numbers, are preferred.

MAY TARPON

Tarpon can be found practically everywhere this month. They are in the passes at low tide (the first bend in the pass is a prime spot), but incoming flow brings them to the back bays. The huge fish are at Homosassa and Boca Grande and all up and down the coast along the beaches. Tarpon fishing in the Keys peaks in May. Some of the finest fly fishing for fish in the sixty- to seventy-pound class, which is the size we prefer, is along the outside of Elliot Key south to the Monroe County line. They are feeding on mullet and catfish, but a ladyfish imitation is especially relished.

MAY REDFISH

Huge reds, up to forty pounds, are around Apalachicola Bay. Here porgy imitations are popular. Twelve- to fifteen-pound redfish are now in the shallow flats all over the state of Florida and around the Gulf coast to Texas. Crab imitations are best, but for the smaller fish, snapping shrimp and scaled sardines work well. The big bull reds take more forage fish than younger reds, which feed mainly on the bottom.

MAY SEA TROUT

Sea trout will be on the grassy flats and oyster bars in the heart of their spawning period. The best fishing is on incoming tides from peak flow to high tide. They will hit just about anything. As of this writing, the Texas coast is best because they have a total net ban.

MAY BONEFISH AND PERMIT

Bonefish are all over the flats from Key West to Biscayne Bay. Permit are mostly offshore, spawning, but there are always some around. The high angle of the sun makes spotting easy. The best fishing is early in the morning or late evening on incoming tides. Use shrimp imitations for bonefish, and blue crabs for permit.

JUNE

June is the transition from spring to summer in latitudes 24° to 26°N. The spring winds have died down, the water is warmer and all of the summer species are active. Even targets like cobia (usually thought of as a deep-water fish caught by bottom fishing outside along structure) can often be found in shallow grass and sand flats in central and north Florida and can be sight-fished.

JUNE SNOOK

This is the prime month when large snook, twenty to fifty pounds and more, can be taken. They are spawning in the passes at night on the full moon, and feeding during the day along the beaches and big mangrove bays just inside the major passes. Early morning is usually best but some of the largest are caught in the afternoon, and night fishing with streamers in the clear grassy bays off the Intercoastal is probably the easiest. They are taking pinfish, threadfins, and scaled sardines. Night fishing under lights around bridges, docks, and piers can be like fishing to a pack of piranha, but here the fish are extremely selective and exact imitations are necessary for success.

JUNE TARPON

All of Florida and select areas in the Bahamas such as the Bights of Andros Island and a few areas in the Berry Islands are surrounded by tarpon in June. From the Florida Keys to the north, tarpon of all sizes are off the beaches and in the passes. They move inside to the bays and river mouths on the high tides. Fish from five to one hundred and fifty pounds and more are moving in and out every day. Late May and June is palolo worm hatch time in the Keys. The worm hatch drives tarpon, bonefish, and permit wild and any reasonable imitation of the orange epitoke (the last few segments of the polo worm full of eggs and sperm) is eagerly taken. This is also the season crabs migrate on the surface through the passes (called pass crabs) at night on strong outgoing tides. A good crab imitation drifted just under the surface is deadly for tarpon, snook, and many other species which are anticipating them around the full and new moons. Other good imitations in June are sand perch, mullet, pinfish, threadfin herring, and scaled sardines.

JUNE REDFISH

In southern Florida, reds will not be as plentiful as in the fall, but there will be some around. In central and northern Florida, Louisiana, Texas, Georgia, and the Carolinas, there will be big reds on the feed. In Florida they will be found on shallow flats and working up the oyster bars on the incoming tides, retreating to the channels and drop-offs on the outgoing tide. Any location that has a net ban will, of course, have more fish. Texas and the backcountry of the Everglade National Park are two examples.

JUNE SEA TROUT

In the southern latitudes, trout will still be around the grassy flats but with the water warming, fishing will taper off. It will be best early in the morning and late afternoon and they will be more plentiful the farther north you go.

JUNE PERMIT AND BONEFISH

In the Keys, permit will be almost done with spawning. From Marathon to the Marquesas, with the calm morning seas of June, sight fishing will be excellent. The same applies to bonefish, and with most guides staked out on bank edges looking for big tarpon, the permit and bonefish flats will have a lot less pressure.

JULY

By many, July is considered the summer doldrums, but if you are flexible there are a lot of opportunities for shallow-water fly fishing. This is also the time of intense offshore angling, so many backcountry flats and bays are deserted. Because of the heat, most fishing slows down in the middle of the day. After the usual afternoon thunderstorms are over, the temperature cools down and our targets go on the feed again. In July, morning, evening, and night fishing are most productive and most tolerable to the angler.

This is the beginning of the rainy season and it brings fresh water into the backcountry. This seems to invigorate backcountry snook. The fresh water stimulates algae bloom so backwaters become darker, which is not all bad since the fish are not as skittish.

JULY SNOOK

The back bays are loaded and the beaches and passes are still full of spawners. Huge feeding snook can be sight-fished along the beaches and the first bays bordering major passes. Best fishing is early morning and late evening. One productive imitation is threadfin herring (pilchard), which school in these areas to feed on the goodies flushed out on strong ebbing tides. Pinfish, needlefish, and scaled sardines are also excellent in the back bays.

JULY TARPON

Tarpon are still plentiful and hungry. They can be found all along the beaches, inside bays, and river mouths. Baby tarpon are abundant up the feeder rivers and streams, especially at the bends. Best fishing is on big-tide periods, but early morning is always good. We like the small #4 to #6 tan or cream Shrimpy at this time.

JULY REDFISH

Many reds begin moving inside from deep waters and fishing gets better as the month progresses. Low to rising tide is great for sight fishing in shallow bays. As the reds move inside, almost any crab, shrimp or baitfish pattern will be taken.

JULY SEA TROUT

Trout fishing gets slow in midsummer, especially in the southern latitudes. The north has more action, and pigfish are a popular imitation. Spawning is mostly over, so where and when you find them they are hungry.

JULY BONEFISH AND PERMIT

Permit are now swarming on offshore wrecks and artificial reefs on the Gulf side. This is not backcountry fishing, but at night they come to the surface to feed and huge permit can be landed on floating crab imitations. Bonefish are best hunted very early and late in the day on the flats, but permit are more tolerant of warm water and quite often can be sighted in the shallows midday.

AUGUST

This month brings the warmest water of the year. It is usually flat calm in the morning and stormy in the afternoon. Backcountry reds and snook fishing slows during August, but outside islands, cuts and bays off major passes hold them and also tarpon. The best fishing is again very early or very late. This is an especially productive month for night fishing, when the temperature is much more pleasant and the fish are more active. The best places are lighted docks, bridges, piers on moving water, and bays along the Intercoastal Waterway.

AUGUST SNOOK

Snook still congregate in the passes and on the beaches and bays along the passes. High tide is best for fishing beaches and flats. On low tide, fish move to deeper holes in the passes and cuts.

AUGUST TARPON

Some areas have plenty of tarpon left, although in many areas they are very scarce. The northwestern part of Florida and the east coast are especially good for tarpon fishing during August. Mullet, menhaden, and pinfish imitations are effective.

AUGUST REDFISH

This should be your target fish during August. Warm water does not seem to bother them as much as other fish, and they are schooled in the flats and first and second inside bays by now in huge numbers. Early or late in the day will be most productive. Mud crabs, scaled sardines, and topwater flies are effective.

AUGUST SEA TROUT

These fish now are not as reliable as earlier. They have left the shallow grass and moved to ten feet of water to escape the heat. Their northern range provides better fishing.

AUGUST BONEFISH AND PERMIT

With the seasonally calm mornings, fish can be seen tailing very early in the day. Although permit like warmer water than bones and can sometimes be taken all day long, fishing is best early and late. The best action is on cloudy days with strong tides.

SEPTEMBER

September is one of the wettest months in Florida, with calm mornings and stormy, wet afternoons. It provides the first hint of seasonal change. Although the days are still very warm, the first cold fronts are hitting Georgia and the Carolinas and this slowly cools the water farther south. It should be the height of the southern mullet migration on the east coast. When they are running, every gamefish will be on the feed. It is also the season when mature white shrimp move from the back nursery bays through the passes and out to open water. Since all gamefish like shrimp, this movement also produces a feeding frenzy.

SEPTEMBER SNOOK

Snook are beginning their movement from the outside passes and bays to the inside. Most will still be on the outside, however, and fishing along the beaches and outside bays is still the main action. Night fishing is productive around lights on bridges and docks close to passes where bay anchovies and scaled sardines swarm.

SEPTEMBER TARPON

All across the state of Florida tarpon will be around the mouths of creeks, rivers, and canals. The same fish which moved north in the spring move south in the fall, only more slowly. It is less concentrated, but the fishing is more reliable. A small tan shrimpy is our first choice for the smaller fish. Use a mullet fly for the 100-plus-pounders.

SEPTEMBER REDFISH

Reds are now schooled in the back bays, grassy flats, and passes and provide very reliable fly fishing. Sight fishing in shallow bays and casting to mangrove islands is the most productive. Try mud crabs and baby mullet imitations.

SEPTEMBER SEA TROUT

Sea trout are mostly in deeper water and will not begin moving to the shallow grass until the water cools. They must be fished with sinking lines.

SEPTEMBER BONEFISH AND PERMIT

More fish will be showing up on the flats as the water cools. It will still be early and late for the best action. If it is cloudy and breezy, fishing will be good in the daytime. Use crabs for permit and mantis or snapping shrimp for bonefish.

OCTOBER

This is the most dynamic month of the year, with water temperatures dropping from 90° and above to 80° or lower. Water temperature is beginning to cool, winds are light, seas are calm, and the water clears up almost everywhere. All of the summer species are still around and the migratory fish such as bluefish and cobia are moving north. Reds, sea trout, and snook are moving from the outside, spreading all over the inside bays, rivers, and creeks. This is one of the very best fly-fishing months both outside and inside.

OCTOBER SNOOK

Snook are slowly moving from the outside spawning areas to the inside wintering areas and putting on fat for the cold weather, when they seldom feed. Good places to start fishing are the middle bays and islands. Pinfish and baby-mullet flies are top producers.

OCTOBER TARPON

Tarpon are moving down the coast on the east side, still feeding on the mullet run. In Florida Bay and the 10,000 Islands there are still plenty around in the mouth of just about any river, creek, or pass. Try shrimp and mullet patterns.

OCTOBER REDFISH

Reds are fully schooled on shallow bays and October is a great month for sight-fishing tailing fish with the clear water and calm winds. Any good crab, shrimp, or baitfish fly will produce.

OCTOBER SEA TROUT

Trout are moving toward the shallows. In the south it's the beginning of the fall run and they are found mostly on grassy flats, four to six feet deep. These fish will take almost any fly fished topwater, midlevel, or deep.

OCTOBER BONEFISH AND PERMIT

October is one of the very best months for big bonefish and permit. Clear water and calm, cooling days bring fish on the flats and allow successful sight fishing all day long. For bones use a tan or cream Shrimpy. In the Bahamas, try olive and brown snapping shrimp and pink sponge shrimp.

NOVEMBER

The water is cooling even more with calm days and clear water, but this month is good fly fishing unless one of the first hard cold fronts comes in. Then choppy seas and dirty water make it tougher. In November you must fish "weather" as well as "tides." Fish will hit best just before the front comes through and then they shut down completely. After the front passes you should move far inside to the mouths of coastal rivers and creeks where clear water will be coming in.

NOVEMBER SNOOK

Snook are moving inside and are where you find them, from outside passes to coastal rivers, sometimes way upriver. The best places to hunt in November are still the middle bays and cuts. They are feeding on baby mullet and pinfish in the bays, and on bluegills and tilapia up the rivers.

NOVEMBER TARPON

Tarpon are beginning to move to warmer water, up rivers or to the open Gulf.

NOVEMBER REDFISH

Reds are still prowling through flats and moving up tidal creeks. By now, the big schools have broken up, so you should look for pods of six or eight fish. Use the same patterns you liked for snook.

NOVEMBER SEA TROUT

This can become really good after the first cold front. Some fish are moving upstream in rivers and creeks. They are often feeding on the glass-minnow migration.

NOVEMBER BONEFISH AND PERMIT

Permit and bonefishing will be excellent until the first bad cold front sends them to deeper water. A few days of warm weather will bring them back. Permit are harder to find than bonefish, and neither will be as plentiful as earlier. The usual shrimp and crab flies will work best.

NOVEMBER SHEEPSHEAD

Sheepshead are considered a winter species but can be a real sleeper in the backcountry. They are moving on oyster bars now and provide great fishing with small fiddler and mud crabs #6 to #8. They can be seen tailing on mud flats, eating a variety of bottom dwellers.

DECEMBER

This is the month of major inshore movement of snook, small tarpon, reds, sea trout, and sheepshead. They proceed from the outer and middle bays to the big inside bays, the mouths of coastal rivers and up the rivers, sometimes very far up. Small cuts between two inside bays are especially good spots on outgoing tides. All the fish in the bays will wind up in the deeper water of the cut eventually. You should choose bluebird days to fish because winter frost stops feeding.

DECEMBER SNOOK

Fish the mouths of creeks early in the morning on an outgoing tide and under heavy structures. If water goes below 70°, look for warmer water. The few days before the first heavy cold snap are very good. Crayfish, bluegill, tilapia, and glass-minnow flies are most productive as the fish move inshore to fresh water.

DECEMBER TARPON

The large fish are now in deep water offshore or up major rivers and deep inside bays. The smaller fish are at the mouths of creeks, rivers, and up the rivers and canals. All are searching for warmer water.

DECEMBER REDFISH

Reds, snapper, and sheepshead will be found well inside, especially around oyster bars, up streams, and in warm canals. Use the same patterns as you would for snook.

DECEMBER SEA TROUT

Some of the best fishing of the year is in north Florida. The fish are found up clear rivers chasing the glass-minnow migration.

DECEMBER BONEFISH AND PERMIT

These fish will only be found on the flats if a warm spell comes along and the water temperature exceeds 70°.

DECEMBER SHEEPSHEAD

The main concentration is now moving in from the Gulf of Mexico. They provide a good winter substitute for bonefish in the northern backcountry. Cold weather seems to invigorate them. They can be found around river mouths, on oyster bars, docks, sea walls, and jetties. Use crab and shrimp imitations.

Sheepshead are a good
winter fish

JANUARY

This is a cold (relatively speaking), blustery month in these latitudes with strong cold fronts moving through. In a word, look for warm water.

JANUARY SNOOK

You need water warmer than 70° to find snook. They will be living with largemouth bass and bluegills. This often means running far up the coastal rivers. In January, some of the best action is in man-made canals that have warm springs bubbling up. There are lots of these in west-central Florida where the blasting of the limestone opened up the aquifer and warm-water springs seeped in. Snook, small tarpon, reds, sea trout, and other species will be congregated in those same areas. Imitate the freshwater prey that live in these areas.

JANUARY TARPON

Tarpon, some weighing 100 pounds plus, can be caught up large rivers. The Caloosahatchee is one of the best, where they are happily feeding on bluegills.

JANUARY REDFISH

Reds are not schooled in the huge numbers you see in the fall, but small schools and singles can be found in the back mangrove country and up the creeks and rivers. Small crab and baitfish patterns are good producers.

JANUARY SEA TROUT

This is probably the most reliable winter fly fish. They are on the shallow grass flats on warm days and in the deeper channels on cooler, windy days. Shrimp flies fished deep should be your first choice.

JANUARY BONEFISH AND PERMIT

Some fish will come on the flats when the water temperature is 70° or warmer. If the water is 60° to 70°, look for barracuda. These are a great winter fly quarry and can save the day in the Keys. Barracuda like baitfish flies stripped back as fast as possible. On the rare warm days, bones larger than ten pounds are common.

FEBRUARY

The first weeks of February are as cold as it gets in Florida, but the latter part of the month can bring some balmy weather that starts fish moving on the flats and back bays. Fish the warm days before the cold fronts move in.

FEBRUARY SNOOK

Most of the linesides (snook) are still up the coastal rivers and canals. Search out water warmer than 70°, especially water found around underground springs. Look for steam on the surface on cold mornings which will alert you to hotspots. The water seeps out at 72°, and snook and lots of other gamefish will crowd around these warm-water areas. A good way up the river, the food chain is different and snook are feeding on crayfish, bluegills and tilapia.

FEBRUARY TARPON

Find 74° waters and you will find tarpon returning to the Keys, especially around bridges. This is sinking-line fishing and is best at night, but you can get hook-ups in the daytime. The best imitation is a finger mullet.

FEBRUARY REDFISH

Look for singles and also small schools in backcountry on bluebird days. Use three-inch baby-mullet patterns.

FEBRUARY SEA TROUT

Best on warm days on the flats, where they take shrimp well.

FEBRUARY BONEFISH
AND PERMIT

The cold weather has chased these fish off the shallow flats, but let the water temperature get to 70° and the fish will be back fast. Two or three warm days can make a great difference. The Atlantic side is best early in the season. The Content Keys area is also good for bones and permit this month.

SEASONS FOR
MID-ATLANTIC AND
NORTH ATLANTIC
REGIONS

Fly fishing in the Mid-Atlantic and North Atlantic regions is mainly a spring, summer, fall affair with each period possessing its own peculiarities. The main targets for backcountry and on-shore fly fishing changes somewhere in the vicinity of Cape Lookout, North Carolina. From this locale, north to Maine, the targets become striped bass, bluefish, bonito, and little tunny. These are superb fly-rod fish—the stripers and blues are bull-dog-strong and the bonito and little tunny are lightning fast.

Striper fishing begins in April in the southern part of the region with the fish arriving in Cape Cod by mid-May, and a little later along the coast of Maine. The bluefish follow hard on the heels of the stripers. Spring finds the gamesters moving north, all along the coast; this is called the spring migration, and is mostly daytime angling although the bass are often fished at night.

Summertime (July, August) is called the summer dol-drums although nights for stripers are very productive.

Fall (called the fall blitz) produces some of the fastest ac-tion because the fish are feeding heavily as they retrace their spring migration. This is again daylight angling, although night fishing is also productive. September and October are our fa-vorite months for fishing Martha's Vineyard and Long Island Sound.

Bonito and little tunny are summer or early fall fish. Bonito are found in the Carolinas in May, reaching Cape Cod by July. They leave the Cape in early October, when the big cold fronts arrive. Little tunny (called false albacore or albies locally), show up in mid-September pretty much everywhere along the northern coast, and leave about the same time as the bonito. These fish feed all day long, so night fishing is not as important as it is for striped bass. Bonito and albies prefer small, slim bait-fish such as sand eels and silversides. Stripers and blues also eat these swarming forage species, but also like wide-bodied fish such as Atlantic herring and butterfish.

Snook and Tarpon
Water for All Seasons

here are little-known, neglected areas that are terrific for tarpon up to fifty pounds and very large snook. In these spots, neither weather nor tides seem to matter much; certainly they are not the overriding factors we usually experience in backcountry fly fishing. These specific waters are a secret closely guarded by those who have found them. To acquire your own secret spot for all seasons, you will have to do some exploring, and once you have discovered one of these special pieces of water you will also guard the location as closely as the others "in the know."

Your first step will be to acquire a map of the area showing as much detail as possible. The very best are aerial photographic maps with a scale of 1:24,000. These are available from the United States Geological Survey of the Department of The Interior. Local county government offices may also have them. Once you have the map, you start searching for a body of water with specific features. You are looking for a pond, lake, canal, river, or creek which is close to some sort of salt water and has a connection, however slight, to that salt water. This connection can even be invisible (and often is), such as an underground drainage pipe or a low-lying area only flooded occasionally.

The water you are looking for need not be salt water; it can be brackish or totally fresh. It should be deep (although some shallower water can be productive), ideally fifteen to thirty feet. This means it has probably been dredged. This is very important, as the dredging not only produces deeper water but opens up the underground aquifer that produces a flow of 72° water year-round. The temperature is modified by the springs. It stays cooler in summer and warmer in winter. Tarpon and snook love this condition. You might think areas as described above would be rare, and in Cape Cod, they may be. In Florida, though, it is difficult to build anything near the coast without dredging fill from somewhere. Houses on canals along rivers and streams need fill for their lots. Small local airports need fill to build up their runways. Overpasses and interchanges on major highways need tons of fill and they usually get it close by. Even the roadbeds themselves need fill for building and repair. Golf courses built in the area are notorious for holding tarpon in their lakes and ponds and it's not because tarpon like golf balls to feed on. All of this dredging creates thousands of ideal habitats for snook and tarpon, and with a good map it becomes easy to pick likely spots to explore. It will appear impossible for the gamefish to get to some spots, yet they do. Not all will produce explosive fishing, but many will.

For more successful fishing it is helpful to understand a little of the biology of our targets. The gamefish drop their eggs offshore or in the passes. The eggs later hatch and the growing fry swim and are swept inshore by strong incoming tides. They proceed to the extreme backwaters, where some are carried even farther into freshwater ponds and lakes by the highest tides of the year. They do not at all mind the fresh water and they are safe from the vicious predators of the shallow salt waters. Strong spring tides cover land areas which are dry most of the time. This is why we find tarpon and snook far up canals, ponds, and lakes you would swear they could never reach.

Once you have studied your map and decided on a likely spot to explore, a small, light skiff and an inexpensive portable depth finder are all you need to get started. The most productive ponds, lakes, and canals may have deep spots, but usually are deep all over. If your first pick is shallow it still may hold fish but usually will not produce the spectacular angling you are searching for. Depth can be quickly checked with the sonar.

Arrive *early* in the morning, launch the boat, then check the water depth. We will assume you have a lake that is suitable. Look for tarpon rolling away from shore, and snook chasing bait in the shallows. If you don't notice any surface action, start fishing by casting a three-inch needlefish or two-inch Shrimpy to the mangrove shoreline. If snook are present, you will know it before much time has passed. If tarpon are around, they will almost always begin showing before morning is over. If you spot rolling fish, put on a two-inch tan Shrimpy and drift the boat among the school. Cast three or four feet ahead of the first fish that comes in range and retrieve with slow but varied strips.

If your first exploration is not successful, try another area. Once you do succeed in discovering a hotspot—your own closely guarded secret hotspot—it will pay huge dividends in good angling for all seasons.

Tarpon dorsal fin

Selected Bibliography

SCIENCE

Boschung Jr., Herbert T. et al. *The Audubon Society Field Guide to North American Fishes, Whales, and Dolphins*. New York: Alfred A. Knopf, 1983.

Eschmeyer, William N. *A Field Guide to Pacific Coast Fishes of North America*. Boston: Houghton Mifflin, 1983.

Hoese, H. Dickson and Moore, Richard H. *Fishes of the Gulf of Mexico*. College Station, TX: Texas A&M University Press, 1977.

Kaplan, Eugene H. *A Field Guide to Coral Reefs*. Boston: Houghton Mifflin, 1982.

Kaplan, Eugene H. *A Field Guide to Southeastern and Caribbean Seashores*. Boston: Houghton Mifflin, 1988.

Manning, Raymond B. *Stomatopod Crustacea Of The Western Atlantic*. Miami: University of Miami Press, 1969.

Meinkoth, Norman A. *The Audubon Society Field Guide to North American Sea Shore Creatures*. New York: Alfred A. Knopf, 1981.

Page, Lawrence M. and Burr, Brooks M. *A Field Guide to Fresh Water Fishes*. Boston: Houghton Mifflin, 1991.

Robins, C. Richard. *A Field Guide to Atlantic Coast Fishes of North America*. Boston: Houghton Mifflin, 1986.

Walls, Jerry G. *Encyclopedia of Marine Invertebrates*. Neptune, N.J.: T.F.H. Publications, 1982.

Williams, Auston B. *Shrimps, Lobsters, and Crabs of the Atlantic Coast of the Eastern United States, Maine to Florida*. Washington D.C.: Smithsonian Institution Press, 1984.

FISHING

Allen, Farrow and Stewart, Dick. *Flies For Saltwater*. Mountain Pond Publishing, 1992.

Bauer, Erwin A. *The Saltwater Fisherman's Bible*. New York: Doubleday, 1991.

Brown, Dick. *Fly Fishing For Bonefish*. New York: Lyons & Burford, Publishers, 1993.

McClane, A. J. and Gardner, Keith. *Game Fish of North America*. New York: Bonanza Books, 1984.

Kreh, Lefty, and Sosin, Mark. *Fishing the Flats*. New York: Lyons & Burford, Publishers, 1983.

Kreh, Lefty. *Saltwater Fly Patterns*. New York: Lyons & Burford, Publishers, 1995.

Sargent, Frank. *The Snook Book*, 1991, *The Redfish Book*, 1991, *The Tarpon Book*, 1991, *The Trout Book*, 1992. Lakeland, FL: Larsen's Outdoor Publishing.

Tabory, Lou. *Inshore Fly Fishing*. New York: Lyons & Burford, Publishers, 1992.

Wentink, Frank. *Saltwater Fly Tying*. New York: Lyons & Burford, Publishers, 1991.

INDEX